MUSHROOMS & TOADSTOOLS

© AA Media Limited 2011
Written by Andrew Merrick

Produced for AA Publishing by D & N Publishing, Baydon, Wiltshire

Commissioning editor at AA Publishing: Paul Mitchell
Production at AA Publishing: Rachel Davis

Printed and bound in China by C&C Offset Printing Co. Ltd

A CIP catalogue record for this book is available from the British Library.

ISBN 978 0 7495 69273
     978 0 7495 69402 (SS)

Disclaimer
Whilst every effort has been made to point out the known poisonous
species likely to be encountered in Britain and the poisonous species
likely to be confused with edible ones, this book should only be used
as a guide and if collecting to eat then advice from an expert should
always be sought.

Published by AA Publishing, a trading name of AA Media Limited,
whose registered office is Fanum House, Basing View, Basingstoke,
Hampshire RG21 4EA. Registered number 06112600.

A04089
theAA.com/shop

CONTENTS

FUNGI, WHICH INCLUDE mushrooms and toadstools, are extremely diverse and vitally important to life on earth. They are great recyclers, releasing nutrients back into the soil through decomposition. A great number of trees and plants form mutually beneficial relationships with fungi, and we make use of them in numerous ways in our everyday lives.

Many fungi are ephemeral, up and over within a few hours, and quick to take advantage of favourable conditions. Others are more lasting and can persist for decades, adding growth year on year. They can be enigmatic, too, capable of stopping us in our tracks – something weird and wonderful beside the path that challenges us to find out what on earth it is.

The *AA Spotter Guide to Mushrooms & Toadstools* covers the most common and widespread species of fungus. In addition, a few spectacular and unusual species are included to whet the reader's appetite.

A full page is devoted to each species. The text has been written in a concise manner so that as much information as possible can be packed into the space available. Each species entry begins with the common English name and is followed by the species' scientific name. For ease of use, the subsequent text has been divided into sections: **FACT FILE**, which covers the species' size, habitat preferences, distribution status and fruiting season; **IDENTIFICATION**, which describes its appearance and, in some cases, its taste and smell; **COMMENTS**, which mainly describes the typical mode of growth with some clues to help find the species; and **KEY FACT**, which gives tips to help the reader find or identify the species in question, or separate it from a similar, close relative. A photograph accompanies the text for each species.

THE BLUSHER is a common and familiar fungus, showing all the features of a classic toadstool.

SUCCESS IN FINDING mushrooms and toadstools is influenced by a variety of factors: time of year, habitat, recent weather and geographical location.

Most people think of autumn as the season to search for fungi but it is by no means the only time worth looking. In spring, morels and St George's Mushroom fruit; summer prompts the vivid brackets of Chicken of the Woods to sprout on old tree trunks; and in the depths of winter Velvet Shank thrives, somehow surviving one hard frost after another.

Fungi have evolved to take full advantage of all kinds of habitat, from woods, moors and heaths to sand-dunes, pastures and marshes. They occur on a great deal of substrates, too: soil, leaf-litter, woodchips, burnt ground, living and rotting wood, grass, mortar, dung, bone, feathers, insects, and even on other fungi. And some are restricted to a particular host – for example, the Orange Birch Bolete forms a mycorrhizal association only with birch trees. Knowing what substrate or host a particular species prefers can help greatly in both tracking it down and identifying it.

Weather has a great influence on fungi. Rain is especially important and can spur a whole host of species into fruiting, sometimes in huge numbers. Summer heatwaves can have a similar effect – the Rooting Bolete, a species increasing its range northwards, probably due to climate change, fruits in hot weather. Cold snaps, too, seem to trigger some fungi to fruit: Oyster Mushroom and Wood Blewit are commonly encountered in winter.

Other species appear to be restricted geographically, despite similar habitats present elsewhere. A good example is Coral Tooth, a species that likes rotting Beech and Ash but occurs only sporadically across Britain, being absent in many areas, including the whole of Scotland and Wales.

Fungi are constantly under threat from human activity. Habitat loss, pollution, changes in climate, farming practices and woodland management all contribute to their decline. Overpicking might also have an impact, and is banned in some woods in the New Forest. A small mirror is a useful aid that avoids the need to uproot every specimen to inspect the underside.

Another way of helping fungi is to join Plantlife (www.plantlife.org.uk), a charity dedicated to wildflower and fungi conservation, or your local county Wildlife Trust (www.wildlifetrusts.org).

WHAT ARE MUSHROOMS AND TOADSTOOLS?

LIVING ORGANISMS ARE split into five natural kingdoms: animals, plants, bacteria, algae and fungi. Fungi, therefore, are not plants, but are in fact an entirely separate group with their own distinct characteristics.

The basic building blocks of most fungi are hyphae. These thread-like filaments combine to form a spreading network collectively known as a mycelium, which branches out within the substrate in search of food. Hyphae can also combine to form the fruiting body of a mushroom or toadstool, the part of the fungus that is visible above ground and that is most readily recognised. The job of these fruit bodies is to make and disperse millions of spores effectively, of which a few may germinate to form the next generation.

The range and diversity of fungal fruit bodies that have evolved is truly remarkable. The classic mushroom or toadstool is made up of a cap, stem and gills, but there is a great variety of other structures, many grouped and named according to how they look: brackets, corals, puffballs, earthstars, cups, ears, clubs, earthtongues, truffles and jellies, to name but a few.

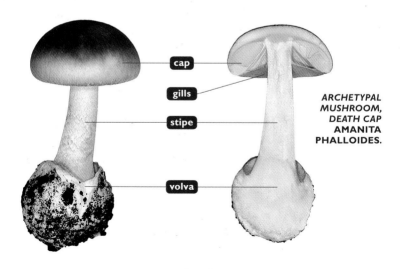

cap

gills

stipe

volva

ARCHETYPAL MUSHROOM, DEATH CAP **AMANITA PHALLOIDES.**

Adnate Gill attached to stem by entire depth of gill.

Adnexed Gill narrow where attached to stem.

Ascomycete Fungus that develops its spores in microscopic flask-like containers known as asci, e.g. the morels.

Basidiomycete Fungus that develops its spores on microscopic club-shaped structures known as basidia, e.g. the Cultivated Mushroom.

Cortina Cobweb-like veil enclosing the gills in some species, especially the webcaps.

Cuticle Outermost layer or skin of the cap.

Decurrent Gill attached to, and running down, the stem.

Deliquesce Turn to a liquid, as seen in the cap and gills of the Shaggy Inkcap.

Free Gill that does not reach the stem and so is not attached to it.

Gill Blade-like structure on which microscopic spore-producing basidia are formed in some basidiomycete fungi.

Hypha (pl. hyphae) Thread-like filament that feeds the fungus.

Mycelium Network of hyphae.

Mycorrhizal Mutually beneficial partnership between a fungus and the roots of a plant.

Pore Open end of a spore-bearing tube, seen in boletes and polypores.

Resupinate Fungus that is entirely pressed flat against the substrate, as if glued on.

Rhizomorph Mycelial cord, formed of hyphae.

Saprotroph Fungus that decomposes dead and decaying matter, releasing nutrients in the process.

Sinuate Gill that is notched just before attachment to the stem.

Spore Microscopic reproductive cell made by the fruit body and capable of germination.

Striate Lined, ridged or grooved, usually referring to the cap margin or stem.

Tube Cylindrical structure on which microscopic spore-producing basidia are formed in some basidiomycete fungi.

Umbo Rounded or pointed projection at the centre of the cap.

Universal veil Protective tissue enclosing the young fruit body that breaks up during growth.

Viscid Lubricious, oily, very slippery.

Volva Bag-like structure at the base of the stem, as found in Deathcap.

PENNY BUN
Boletus edulis

FACT FILE

SIZE **Cap diameter 5–25cm; height 5–15cm**
HABITAT **Associated with deciduous trees and sometimes conifers**
STATUS **Widespread and common** FRUITING SEASON **Aug–Oct**

IDENTIFICATION
Cap is bun-shaped with a greasy surface; mottled reddish brown, paler towards edge, sometimes with a thin white band around margin. Pores are white, yellowing with age. Stem is usually swollen, with a white network on a pale brown background. Flesh is white.

KEY FACT The Summer Bolete *Boletus reticulatus* and *Boletus aereus* are closely related edible summer-fruiting species. The inedible Bitter Bolete *Tylopilus felleus* differs in having pink pores and a dark brown network on the stem.

COMMENTS
A highly prized edible, well known across Europe as Cep or Porcini. It fruits in autumn and can be found under deciduous trees almost anywhere.

SPOTTER'S CHART

LOCATION	DATE/TIME

FACT FILE

SIZE Cap diameter 5–20cm; height 4–10cm
HABITAT Associated with deciduous trees STATUS Widespread and common in S England FRUITING SEASON Jul–Sep

KEY FACT

This species has been increasing in S Britain in recent years, probably due to the ever warmer climate. The similar Oak Bolete *Boletus appendiculatus* differs in having a reddish-brown cap.

SPOTTER'S CHART

LOCATION	DATE/TIME

IDENTIFICATION

Cap is bun-shaped, uniformly grey. Pores are yellow but blue when bruised. Stem is pale to lemon yellow, often with a reddish band around middle and an indistinct yellow network near top. Flesh is pale yellow, turning blue when cut or bruised.

COMMENTS

Regularly encountered fruiting in groups on road verges under large oaks and Beech during late summer and early autumn. It is more scarce in the N.

BAY BOLETE
Boletus badius

SIZE Cap diameter 5–15cm; height 4–12cm
HABITAT Coniferous and, less commonly, deciduous woodland
STATUS Widespread and common **FRUITING SEASON** Aug–Nov

IDENTIFICATION
Cap is bun-shaped, flattening with age; surface is slimy or dry, light bay to chestnut. Pores are pale olive-yellow when mature, bruising blue. Stem is streaked with fine brownish fibrils on a pale yellow background. Flesh is white to pale yellow, not discolouring when cut or bruised.

KEY FACT
Edible and fairly easy to identify with a little practice, especially if you allow for a dry or slimy cap surface. Overall, the cap and stem contrast well with the olive-yellow pores, which bruise blue.

COMMENTS
Generally associated with conifers, though it is regularly found under deciduous trees without a conifer in sight.

SPOTTER'S CHART

LOCATION	DATE/TIME

FACT FILE

SIZE Cap diameter 4–8cm; height 4–8cm
HABITAT Associated with deciduous and coniferous trees
STATUS Widespread and common FRUITING SEASON Jul–Nov

IDENTIFICATION

Cap is rounded, expanding and flattening; surface is finely velvety, becoming finely cracked to reveal pinkish flesh beneath. Pores are bright yellow, becoming olive and slowly bruising blue. Stem is slender; yellow at top, red below and wine red at base; flesh in base turns blue when cut.

KEY FACT

A newly described species, only recently separated from the better known *Boletus chrysenteron*. It differs from the latter by the more extensive cracking on the cap surface and the strong blue discoloration of the flesh in the stem base soon after it is cut.

COMMENTS

Forms a mycorrhizal partnership with the roots of various tree species, especially hardwoods such as oaks and Beech. Rarely recorded under conifers.

SPOTTER'S CHART

LOCATION	DATE/TIME

MATT BOLETE
Boletus pruinatus

FACT FILE

SIZE Cap diameter 3–10cm; height 3–10cm
HABITAT Deciduous woodland, especially Beech; rarely with conifers
STATUS Local and occasional   FRUITING SEASON Sep–Nov

IDENTIFICATION
Cap is rounded, expanding and flattening; surface is waxy or suede-like, deep red-brown to date brown, visibly covered in a white bloom, especially when young. Pores are bright lemon yellow, barely discolouring blue when bruised. Stem is slender; bright yellow, sometimes dotted with red. Flesh is lemon yellow.

COMMENTS
Typically found fruiting singly or in small groups in leaf-litter under Beech in late autumn and often well into Nov. It is edible but not worthwhile.

KEY FACT

The generally late appearance of this species, along with its non-cracking cap and bright yellow stem flesh should help separate it from similar species such as the Red-cracking Bolete.

SPOTTER'S CHART

LOCATION	DATE/TIME

FACT FILE SIZE Cap diameter 7–20cm; height 8–20cm
HABITAT **Always associated with birch trees** STATUS **Widespread
and very common** FRUITING SEASON Jul–Nov

IDENTIFICATION

Cap is bun-shaped, expanding
and flattening; surface is finely
felty, light to mid-orange, margin
slightly overhanging pores. Pores
are light greyish. Stem is thick,
covered in small blackish scales
on a white background. Flesh is
white, turning wine red and
finally blackish with a blue-green
discoloration in stem base.

COMMENTS

Forms a mycorrhizal partnership
with the roots of birch trees in
damp woodland and heathland,
where it is commonly found
fruiting in the autumn.

KEY FACT Orange Oak
Bolete *Leccinum aurantiacum* is
similar but mainly associated
with oaks and poplars, and the
stem is densely covered in rusty
scales on a white background.
The completely white-stemmed
Leccinum albostipitatum grows
under Aspen and poplars.

SPOTTER'S CHART

LOCATION	DATE/TIME

BROWN BIRCH BOLETE
Leccinum scabrum

FACT FILE

SIZE Cap diameter 5–15cm; height 8–18cm
HABITAT Always associated with birch trees **STATUS** Widespread
and common **FRUITING SEASON** Jul–Nov

IDENTIFICATION
Cap is bun-shaped, soon soft and somewhat tacky, light brown to nearly
black. Pores are white, becoming more dingy with age. Stem is white
to greyish, covered in dark brown
scales, these denser towards base.
Flesh is white, discolouring pinkish
or not at all, and with no blue
staining in stem base.

KEY FACT
Once split into
a number of separate species,
this is now generally regarded as
a single highly variable species.
The Mottled Bolete *Leccinum
variicolor* is similar but with a
mottled cap and blue-green
stains in the lower stem.

COMMENTS
Forms a mycorrhizal partnership
with the roots of birch trees and
can be found fruiting under them
in late summer and autumn.

SPOTTER'S CHART

LOCATION	DATE/TIME

FACT FILE

SIZE **Cap diameter 5–10cm; height 6–10cm**
HABITAT **Always associated with pines** STATUS **Widespread and very common** FRUITING SEASON **Jul–Oct**

IDENTIFICATION

Cap is convex, often with a slight umbo; surface is fibrillose, very slimy, light to dark reddish brown. Pores are yellow but covered by a partial veil when young. Ring is broad, fairly fleeting; white, developing purple tints. Stem is pale yellow and dotted brown above ring, white below.

COMMENTS

Sometimes abundant under pines in the autumn, Slippery Jack is edible but best avoided as known to cause gastric upsets in some, especially if the cap cuticle is not removed first.

KEY FACT

Weeping Bolete *Suillus granulatus* and the rare *S. collinitus* are similar but neither has a stem ring. In addition, the Weeping Bolete often exudes milky drops from its pore surface and upper stem.

SPOTTER'S CHART

LOCATION	DATE/TIME

BOVINE BOLETE
Suillus bovinus

FACT FILE

SIZE Cap diameter 3–10cm; height 3–6cm
HABITAT Always associated with pines STATUS Widespread
and very common FRUITING SEASON Jul–Oct

IDENTIFICATION
Cap is convex, flattening; surface is slimy when wet, drying smooth; pale
to dark ochre, often with a white margin. Pores are adnate to decurrent,
some quite large and angular, olivaceous. Stem is usually a shade lighter
than cap and often curved at base. Flesh is white to pale yellow.

KEY FACT
The beautiful
Rosy Spike *Gomphidius roseus*
can often be found growing
alongside this species and is
thought to be parasitic on both
it and the associated pines.

SPOTTER'S CHART

LOCATION	DATE/TIME

COMMENTS
Usually grows in clusters under
pines, especially on poor acid soils.
Although edible, it has a slightly
sour taste.

FACT FILE

SIZE Cap diameter 5–15cm; height 5–12cm
HABITAT Rich soil in deciduous woods, especially oak and Beech
STATUS Widespread and occasional FRUITING SEASON Jul–Oct

IDENTIFICATION

Cap is convex with a depressed centre and inrolled margin, becoming funnel-shaped when mature; surface is matt, dry, whitish. Gills are decurrent, very narrow and very crowded, cream. Stem is white, tapering towards base, smooth and dry. Flesh is very acrid, as is the milk after a while.

SPOTTER'S CHART

LOCATION	DATE/TIME

COMMENTS

Edible but not worthwhile owing to its very hot, peppery taste, though this is reduced or even removed by cooking.

KEY FACT

Similar in appearance to the Fleecy Milkcap *Lactarius vellereus*, but that species has a velvety cap, less crowded gills and milk that tastes mild when isolated from the acrid flesh.

WOOLLY MILKCAP
Lactarius torminosus

FACT FILE

SIZE Cap diameter 5–10cm; height 4–8cm
HABITAT Always associated with birches on dry or damp soils
STATUS Widespread and common **FRUITING SEASON** Jul–Oct

IDENTIFICATION

Cap is convex with a depressed centre, margin remaining inrolled for a long time; surface is smooth in centre and increasingly hairy towards margin, with concentric light and dark zones. Gills are slightly decurrent, crowded, pale pinkish. Stem is cylindrical, smooth, salmon coloured. Milk is white and hot.

KEY FACT

The Bearded Milkcap *Lactarius pubescens* also grows with birch trees but differs in having a much paler, less hairy cap without the light and dark concentric zones.

COMMENTS

Usually found growing in groups and always in the vicinity of birches. It is best avoided as it has been known to cause severe vomiting in some people.

SPOTTER'S CHART

LOCATION	DATE/TIME

YELLOWDROP MILKCAP
Lactarius chrysorrheus

FACT FILE

SIZE **Cap diameter 3–8cm; height 2–5cm**
HABITAT **Almost always associated with oaks**
STATUS **Widespread and common** FRUITING SEASON **Aug–Oct**

IDENTIFICATION
Cap is convex, often with a depressed centre when older; surface is salmon-buff with darker ring zones that sometimes comprise spots. Gills are adnate to slightly decurrent, crowded, cream to pinkish buff. Stem is smooth; whitish, discolouring with age. Milk is white then yellow. Flesh is acrid.

COMMENTS
Considered by some to be poisonous, the species is certainly inedible when raw on account of the acrid-tasting flesh.

KEY FACT
As its name suggests, the most distinctive feature of this species is the yellowing milk, which is copiously exuded from the gills when damaged. Initially white, the milk soon becomes bright yellow.

SPOTTER'S CHART

LOCATION	DATE/TIME

SAFFRON MILKCAP
Lactarius deliciosus

SIZE **Cap diameter 4–10cm; height 3–7cm**
HABITAT **Always associated with pines** STATUS **Widespread and common** FRUITING SEASON **Sep–Oct**

IDENTIFICATION
Cap is initially convex with an inrolled margin, later expanding with a depressed centre; surface is pale salmon with darker specks forming concentric zones, often with some greening. Gills are decurrent, crowded, salmon with a paler edge. Stem is short and fat, pitted; salmon, bruising greenish. Milk and flesh are carrot coloured.

COMMENTS
Widely distributed and often abundant wherever pines occur. It is a good edible and much prized and collected, especially on the Continent.

KEY FACT
The similar **False Saffron Mikcap** *Lactarius deterrimus* grows under spruce. The rare *L. semisanguifluus* does grow under pines but is smaller, readily turns green all over and has lilac tints in the cap.

SPOTTER'S CHART

LOCATION	DATE/TIME

FACT FILE

SIZE **Cap diameter 4–9cm; height 3–7cm**

HABITAT **Mainly under Beech, more rarely with other deciduous trees**

STATUS **Widespread and very common** FRUITING SEASON **Jul–Nov**

IDENTIFICATION

Cap is convex with an inrolled margin, later expanding with a depressed centre; surface is slimy when wet, pale olive-grey to dark olive-grey, sometimes with concentric bands of spots. Gills are slightly decurrent, crowded, whitish. Stem is slimy, paler than cap. Flesh is acrid. Milk is white, drying grey-green.

KEY FACT The scientific name *blennius* means slimy, and the species is sometimes known as the Slimy Milkcap, which it invariably is in wet weather, although this is less evident when conditions are dry.

COMMENTS

A very common species, growing singly or, more often, in large groups in leaf-litter, especially under pure stands of Beech in the autumn.

SPOTTER'S CHART

LOCATION	DATE/TIME

GREY MILKCAP
Lactarius vietus

SIZE Cap diameter 2–7cm; height 3–7cm
HABITAT Associated with birches in damp areas
STATUS Widespread and common **FRUITING SEASON** Aug–Oct

IDENTIFICATION
Cap is initially convex with an inrolled margin, becoming centrally depressed or funnelled; surface is smooth, pale greyish buff, viscid. Gills are decurrent, crowded, cream. Stem is smooth, cream to greyish, sometimes with a paler zone at apex. Milk is white, drying greenish grey; very hot.

COMMENTS
An inedible species with a distinct preference for growing in *Sphagnum* moss and always in the vicinity of birch trees, with which it forms a mycorrhizal partnership.

KEY FACT
An easily overlooked species on account of its dull greyish colours. However, if its typical habitat and greenish-grey drying milk are kept in mind, finding and identifying the species is made a little easier.

SPOTTER'S CHART

LOCATION	DATE/TIME

FACT FILE

SIZE **Cap diameter 3–8cm; height 3–7cm**
HABITAT **Always associated with oaks** STATUS **Widespread and common** FRUITING SEASON **Jul–Oct**

IDENTIFICATION

Cap is convex with a slightly inrolled margin, later flattening; surface is dry, smooth; pale orange-buff, darker in centre, paler at margin, often with darker concentric zones. Gills are adnate, crowded, pale creamy buff. Stem is cylindrical, smooth, dry; concolourous with cap, darkening with age. Milk is white, mild.

COMMENTS

An inedible species growing singly or in quite large, scattered groups under oak trees, with which it forms a mycorrhizal partnership.

KEY FACT

A good aid to identification is the species' strong oily smell, said to be reminiscent of bed bugs or of the pungent liquid emitted by some pentatomid bugs such as the aptly name stink bugs.

SPOTTER'S CHART

LOCATION	DATE/TIME

BLACKENING BRITTLEGILL
Russula nigricans

FACT FILE

SIZE Cap diameter 8–16cm; height 4–8cm
HABITAT Mainly in mixed deciduous woodland **STATUS** Widespread
and very common **FRUITING SEASON** Jul–Nov

IDENTIFICATION

Cap is convex with an inrolled margin, becoming centrally depressed; surface is smooth, dry, firm; dirty white, then with brown patches and finally blackening. Gills are thick and widely spaced, white to buff, bruising reddish. Stem is short, fat, dense and brittle; white, bruising red and then turning black.

KEY FACT

Look out for small greyish-white fungi growing on the caps of the rotting fruit bodies of this species. They are likely to be one of the two species of piggyback or *Asterophora* fungi.

COMMENTS

A very common species, typically encountered in groups and often persisting for a year or more in a shrivelled, blackened state.

SPOTTER'S CHART

LOCATION	DATE/TIME

FACT FILE

SIZE **Cap diameter 8–10cm; height 6–8cm**
HABITAT **Deciduous and coniferous woodland** STATUS **Widespread and very common** FRUITING SEASON **Jul–Oct**

IDENTIFICATION
Cap is rounded, expanding and flattening, margin often inrolled for some time; surface is smooth and dry, evenly yellow or greenish yellow. Gills are adnexed, fairly crowded, brittle, cream. Stem is cylindrical; whitish, becoming greyer with age. Flesh is white, tastes mild to slightly acrid.

KEY FACT The cap is often partly covered with adhering dead leaves, so it blends in with the forest floor and can be hard to spot. The species is a favourite food of slugs and squirrels, so undamaged specimens are hard to find.

COMMENTS
In most years the Ochre Brittlegill is common, although it can be hard to find following periods of dry weather.

SPOTTER'S CHART

LOCATION	DATE/TIME

YELLOW SWAMP BRITTLEGILL
Russula claroflava

FACT FILE

SIZE Cap diameter 4–8cm; height 3–8cm
HABITAT In wet areas under birches STATUS Widespread
and common FRUITING SEASON Aug–Oct

IDENTIFICATION

Cap is domed, becoming flatter as it matures but staying rounded for some time; surface is smooth, evenly lemon to golden yellow. Gills are adnexed; whitish, becoming more cream, ageing and bruising dark grey. Stem is cylindrical; white, becoming dark grey. Taste is mild and odour not distinctive.

KEY FACT

The deep yellow colour of the cap, together with the greying bruised or ageing flesh, help identify this species. The similar Ochre Brittlegill has a duller cap and prefers a drier habitat.

COMMENTS

Typically found growing in small groups in *Sphagnum* moss under birch trees, with which it forms a mycorrhizal partnership.

SPOTTER'S CHART

LOCATION	DATE/TIME

CHARCOAL BURNER

Russula cyanoxantha

FACT FILE

SIZE **Cap diameter 4–14cm; height 3–10cm**

HABITAT **Mixed deciduous woodland; less frequently under conifers**

STATUS **Widespread and common** FRUITING SEASON **Jul–Oct**

KEY FACT A very variable species, especially in cap colour, with many varieties and forms described. For example, a not uncommon all-green-capped form has been named *peltereaui*.

IDENTIFICATION

Cap is broadly rounded, sometimes with a slight depression; surface is smooth, with varying amounts of violet and green, usually darker in centre. Gills are crowded, flexible and somewhat greasy. Stem is robust, cylindrical; white, sometimes flushed with lilac.

COMMENTS

Gills that flex without breaking is a key feature and a good indication of this species (most other related species have brittle gills).

SPOTTER'S CHART

LOCATION	DATE/TIME

BIRCH BRITTLEGILL
Russula betularum

FACT FILE

SIZE **Cap diameter 2–5cm; height 2–6cm**
HABITAT **Always under birch trees** STATUS **Widespread and common** FRUITING SEASON **Aug–Oct**

IDENTIFICATION
Cap is very fragile; pink, often with light and dark patches, soon becoming washed out to almost white, especially in centre; cuticle peels almost entirely. Gills are well spaced, white. Stem is cylindrical, slender and fragile, white. Tastes very hot; smells faintly of coconut.

KEY FACT The small size, pink cap and very hot-tasting flesh all help in identifying this delicate species. *Russula exalbicans* is another pink-capped birch associate, but is much larger and has very crowded gills.

COMMENTS
A common species that forms a mycorrhizal partnership with birch trees and is often encountered fruiting abundantly beneath them.

SPOTTER'S CHART

LOCATION	DATE/TIME

FACT FILE

SIZE **Cap diameter 4–10cm; height 3–8cm**
HABITAT **Mainly associated with conifers in damp areas**
STATUS **Widespread and very common** FRUITING SEASON **Aug–Nov**

IDENTIFICATION

Cap is rounded, becoming flatter; shiny, scarlet to blood red; cuticle peels almost completely. Gills are adnate and medium-spaced, white. Stem is often more swollen towards top, brittle, white. Smells fruity, with a hint of coconut.

COMMENTS

A very common species that forms a mycorrhizal partnership with Scots Pine and spruce trees throughout the British Isles, especially in damper areas with *Sphagnum* moss.

KEY FACT

As its common and scientific names suggest, this is an inedible species known to have caused various gastro-intestinal complaints. The similar Beechwood Sickener *Russula nobilis* grows in association with Beech.

SPOTTER'S CHART

LOCATION	DATE/TIME

PRIMROSE BRITTLEGILL
Russula sardonia

FACT FILE

SIZE **Cap diameter 4–12cm; height 3–8cm**
HABITAT **Associated with pines** STATUS **Widespread
and common** FRUITING SEASON **Aug–Nov**

IDENTIFICATION
Cap is broadly domed and
fleshy, typically purplish
red to wine red but other
colour forms occur rarely;
cuticle hardly peels. Gills
are adnate to slightly
decurrent, pale lemon
yellow. Stem is cylindrical,
firm, often flushed pinkish
red. Tastes very hot;
smells fruity.

COMMENTS
Although restricted to
pines, Primrose Brittlegill is
nonetheless very common
wherever they occur and can
often be found fruiting in quite
large numbers.

KEY FACT
The lemon-
tinted gills are an important
field character in identifying the
species. The rare *Russula torulosa*
has cream gills with no hint
of yellow and occurs under
Corsican Pine in coastal districts.

SPOTTER'S CHART

LOCATION	DATE/TIME

PURPLE BRITTLEGILL
Russula atropurpurea

FACT FILE

SIZE **Cap diameter 4–12cm; height 3–9cm**
HABITAT **Mixed woodland, especially with oaks** STATUS **Widespread and very common** FRUITING SEASON **Aug–Nov**

IDENTIFICATION

Cap is rounded, sometimes with a slight central depression; blood red to purple, blacker at centre; cuticle peels a third to halfway. Gills are crowded, white. Stem is cylindrical, robust; white, discolouring greyish with age. Tastes mild but may be hot in gills; smells fruity.

COMMENTS

Edible but not worthwhile. If eaten, it should be parboiled first to remove any acrid taste.

KEY FACT

An important character for identifying brittlegills is how much the thin cap cuticle can be peeled back from the margin before breaking. Peeling to halfway means halfway between the cap margin and cap centre.

SPOTTER'S CHART

LOCATION	DATE/TIME

PARASOL
Macrolepiota procera

FACT FILE

SIZE Cap diameter 10–25cm; height 10–40cm
HABITAT Grassland, open woodland, sand-dunes
STATUS Widespread and common **FRUITING SEASON** Aug–Nov

IDENTIFICATION
Cap is egg-shaped at first, becoming convex to planar with a central umbo; surface is covered in quite large brown scales, concentrically arranged on a much paler background. Gills are white and crowded. Stem is tall, bulbous at base and usually with conspicuous brown snakeskin banding. Ring is double-edged.

KEY FACT
Confusion with the Shaggy Parasol is possible, but that species prefers more shady, wooded places on rich soil. The Shaggy Parasol also lacks the snakeskin banding on the stem.

COMMENTS
An excellent edible, typically found growing in groups in open grassy areas or edges of woodland, especially on sandy soil.

SPOTTER'S CHART

LOCATION	DATE/TIME

FACT FILE

SIZE Cap diameter 8–18cm; height 8–20cm
HABITAT Deciduous and coniferous woodland, parks and gardens
STATUS Widespread and common **FRUITING SEASON** Jul–Dec

IDENTIFICATION

Cap is egg-shaped at first, becoming convex to planar with large brown upturned scales on a creamy white background. Gills are white to cream and free from stem. Stem is smooth, with a distinctly bulbous base; white, bruising brownish. Ring is large and double-edged, located high on stem and movable.

KEY FACT

Edible, but should always be cooked well first as it contains toxins that can cause stomach upsets in some people. Most commonly confused with the Parasol, which is taller, has a snakeskin pattern on the stem and prefers more open, grassy places.

COMMENTS

Typically found growing in fairy rings in quite shaded situations on rich soil, especially in woods and on road verges, throughout the autumn.

SPOTTER'S CHART

LOCATION	DATE/TIME

STINKING DAPPERLING
Lepiota cristata

FACT FILE

SIZE **Cap diameter 2–7cm; height 3–7cm**
HABITAT **Rich soil in deciduous and coniferous woods**
STATUS **Widespread and common** FRUITING SEASON **Jul–Dec**

IDENTIFICATION
Cap is convex to planar with a low umbo; reddish brown in centre, disrupting into concentric rings of lighter brown scales on a silky white background away from centre. Gills are free and white. Stem is silky white, fibrillose, with a delicate ring that is often fleeting or torn. Smells unpleasantly of chemicals.

KEY FACT
As its common name suggests, this species has a strong, unpleasant gas-like smell that is a useful identification aid. However, some very similar *Lepiota* species occur in the same habitats.

COMMENTS
Typically found growing singly or in small groups on rich soil under trees, shrubs and Common Nettle patches on pathsides and road verges in autumn.

SPOTTER'S CHART

LOCATION	DATE/TIME

FACT FILE SIZE Cap diameter 8–20cm; height 8–20cm
HABITAT Associated with birches on acid soils STATUS Widespread
and very common FRUITING SEASON Sep–Nov

IDENTIFICATION

Cap is hemispherical, gradually expanding and flattening; surface is bright red with many white wart-like fragments that are easily washed off. Gills are free and white. Stem is cylindrical, with a membranous ring and a large basal bulb ringed with tufts of white scales.

KEY FACT The white warty fragments on the cap surface are formed as the universal veil encapsulating the young fruit body expands and breaks up. These warts give the Fly Agaric a very distinctive look, but may be washed off in heavy rain.

COMMENTS

A well-known poisonous hallucinogenic species that is nearly always found under birches, with which it forms a mycorrhizal partnership.

SPOTTER'S CHART

LOCATION	DATE/TIME

BLUSHER
Amanita rubescens

FACT FILE

SIZE Cap diameter 5–15cm; height 5–15cm
HABITAT Mainly with deciduous trees especially birches
STATUS Widespread and very common **FRUITING SEASON** Jun–Nov

IDENTIFICATION

Cap is hemispherical, gradually expanding and flattening; surface is reddish brown with many cream to reddish-brown fragments that are easily washed off. Gills are free; white, bruising reddish. Stem is cylindrical with a large basal bulb and striate ring; white, though often slightly flushed red.

KEY FACT
The Blusher's common name arose because all parts turn slowly red when bruised or damaged. This character, together with the striate ring, helps distinguish it from close relatives such as the Panther Cap.

COMMENTS

Very common under birch trees, often appearing in midsummer immediately after rain.

SPOTTER'S CHART

LOCATION	DATE/TIME

FACT FILE

SIZE Cap diameter 4–12cm; height 4–15cm
HABITAT Mainly associated with oaks and Beech **STATUS** Occasional;
more prevalent in the S **FRUITING SEASON** Aug–Oct

IDENTIFICATION

Cap is egg-shaped, expanding and flattening with age; radially fibrillose,
yellowish olive-green. Gills are free, white. Stem is cylindrical with a
zigzag pattern and a basal bulb enclosed in a papery sac-like volva. Smell
is strong, sickly sweet and honey-like in older specimens but faint or
absent in younger ones.

COMMENTS

Forms a mycorrhizal
partnership with the roots of
Beech and oak trees, including
the Holm Oak, and can be
found fruiting singly or in
small groups beneath them.

KEY FACT

Deadly poisonous,
but is not easily confused with
edible species if the combination of
smell, cap colour and presence of a
volval bag and floppy ring are noted.
A pure white-capped form is known.

SPOTTER'S CHART

LOCATION	DATE/TIME

PANTHERCAP
Amanita pantherina

FACT FILE

SIZE Cap diameter 5–15cm; height 5–15cm
HABITAT Mixed deciduous woodland especially oaks and Beech
STATUS Widespread and occasional FRUITING SEASON Sep–Oct

IDENTIFICATION

Cap is hemispherical, gradually expanding and flattening; surface is brown with a striate margin and many white wart-like fragments that are easily washed off. Gills are free, white. Stem is cylindrical with a large basal bulb that has a distinctive rim at top, and a white ring without striations. Smells of raw potatoes.

KEY FACT

Very poisonous as well as hallucinogenic. Key features are the rim around the bulbous stem base, stem ring without striations, pure white warts on a brown cap, and smell of raw potatoes.

COMMENTS

Forms a mycorrhizal partnership with the roots of various deciduous trees, principally oaks and Beech.

SPOTTER'S CHART

LOCATION	DATE/TIME

FALSE DEATHCAP
Amanita citrina

FACT FILE

SIZE **Cap diameter 3–10cm; height 4–12cm**
HABITAT **Mixed deciduous woodland, especially birches**
STATUS **Widespread and very common** FRUITING SEASON **Jul–Nov**

KEY FACT

The False Deathcap can vary in appearance quite considerably. If it has been raining then the cap may be pale and lack velar remnants, although equally this might be the pure white var. *alba*.

IDENTIFICATION

Cap is hemispherical, gradually expanding and flattening; surface is pale yellow with a hint of green, sometimes pure white (var. *alba*), covered in large, irregular patches of universal veil that are easily washed off. Gills are free and white. Stem is cylindrical with a basal bulb and white ring.

COMMENTS

Not poisonous but best avoided owing to the unpleasant raw potato-like smell and similarity to the Deathcap.

SPOTTER'S CHART

LOCATION	DATE/TIME

GRISETTE
Amanita vaginata

FACT FILE

SIZE Cap diameter 3–8cm; height 8–15cm
HABITAT Mixed deciduous woodland, especially under Beech and oaks
STATUS Widespread and occasional **FRUITING SEASON** Aug–Oct

KEY FACT One of a number of *Amanita* species whose lack of a stem ring serves as a useful character in separating it from many others that do. The Tawny Grisette is very similar but has a greyish, not fulvous, cap colour.

IDENTIFICATION
Cap is egg-shaped to conical, expanding and flattening with a small central umbo; surface is grey to grey-brown with a distinctly striate margin. Gills are white and free. Stem is whitish, tapering upwards and with a large volval bag at base; ring is absent.

COMMENTS
A tall, slender species found fruiting singly or in small scattered groups under various trees in mixed deciduous woodland.

SPOTTER'S CHART

LOCATION	DATE/TIME

FACT FILE

SIZE Cap diameter 3–8cm; height 6–15cm
HABITAT Mainly deciduous woodland and heaths under birches
STATUS Widespread and very common **FRUITING SEASON** Jun–Nov

IDENTIFICATION

Cap is egg-shaped at first, expanding and flattening with a small umbo; orange-brown with a distinctly grooved margin. Gills are free and white. Stem is cylindrical, long and slender with a basal sac-like volva; white with a hint of cap colour; ring is absent.

KEY FACT

Edible, but needs to be cooked first as it is known to cause stomach upsets. It is best avoided owing to possible confusion with some poisonous relatives such as the Deathcap, though the lack of a stem ring is a useful characteristic in that regard.

COMMENTS

Very common and especially abundant shortly after heavy rain. It is best looked for wherever birches grow, although it is not restricted to them.

SPOTTER'S CHART

LOCATION	DATE/TIME

SCARLET WAXCAP
Hygrocybe coccinea

FACT FILE

SIZE **Cap diameter 2–5cm; height 2–6cm**
HABITAT **Mainly unimproved grassland, including lawns**
STATUS **Widespread and common** FRUITING SEASON **Oct–Nov**

KEY FACT
Waxcaps typically grow in unimproved grassland that has not been ploughed or fertilised for a long time. The number of species occurring in these grasslands is used as a measure of quality, with the best sites supporting in excess of 30 waxcap species.

IDENTIFICATION
Cap is hemispherical, slippery but not slimy except after rain, scarlet to blood red but can become washed out. Gills are broadly adnate, red with a yellow edge. Stem is cylindrical to somewhat compressed, dry, concolourous with cap or slightly paler.

SPOTTER'S CHART

LOCATION	DATE/TIME

COMMENTS
Normally found fruiting in groups with other species of waxcap in unimproved grassland, including lawns, cricket pitches and playing fields.

FACT FILE

SIZE **Cap diameter 2–6cm; height 2–8cm**

HABITAT **Mainly unimproved grassland, including lawns and sand-dunes**

STATUS **Widespread and common** FRUITING SEASON **Oct–Nov**

IDENTIFICATION

Cap is hemispherical, later flattening, sometimes with a broad but shallow umbo; slimy; lemon to orange-yellow. Gills are adnexed, pale to mid-yellow. Stem is cylindrical to somewhat compressed, dry and smooth, concolourous with cap although base is often paler.

KEY FACT

There are a number of other yellow waxcaps that could be confused with this species, but the combination of slimy cap, dryish stem and adnexed gills should help to identify it.

COMMENTS

As with many other waxcaps, this one is most at home in unimproved grassland that has been kept short by mowing or grazing.

SPOTTER'S CHART

LOCATION	DATE/TIME

MEADOW WAXCAP
Hygrocybe pratensis

FACT FILE

SIZE Cap diameter 4–10cm; height 3–12cm
HABITAT Mainly unimproved grassland, including lawns
STATUS Widespread and common FRUITING SEASON Aug–Nov

IDENTIFICATION
Cap is hemispherical at first, flattening, sometimes becoming upturned at the margin, occasionally with a broad umbo; dry; pale apricot colour. Gills are deeply decurrent, distant, cream to pale orange. Stem is cylindrical, tapering near base; dry and fibrillose; cream with a hint of cap colour.

SPOTTER'S CHART

LOCATION	DATE/TIME

KEY FACT
The waxcaps are not noted for their culinary qualities, but this species is the exception and is probably the only worthwhile member of the group. The apricot-coloured cap and deeply decurrent gills are the key characters.

COMMENTS
One of our largest and commonest waxcaps, and able to tolerate lower-quality grassland than many other species.

IDENTIFICATION
Cap is narrowly conical at first, expanding but remaining conical with
an umbo; colour is very variable but mostly yellow, orange or red. Gills
are adnexed or free, whitish to yellowish. Stem is cylindrical, fibrillose
and dry. All parts blacken with age or handling.

KEY FACT Many varieties of the
species have been described, including
var. *conicoides*, which has a red cap and
grows in fixed coastal sand-dunes.

COMMENTS
Grows in a wide range of
habitats and is very variable,
but always retains the key
features of a conical cap
and blackening with age
or handling.

SPOTTER'S CHART

LOCATION	DATE/TIME

SNOWY WAXCAP
Hygrocybe virginea

FACT FILE

SIZE Cap diameter 2–6cm; height 2–7cm
HABITAT Grasslands, lawns, fixed sand-dunes STATUS Widespread
and very common FRUITING SEASON Sep–Nov

IDENTIFICATION
Cap is hemispherical, flattening
and sometimes with an upturned
margin; ivory white when fresh,
becoming white when dry;
slippery when moist. Gills are
deeply to shortly decurrent,
white. Stem is cylindrical, often
slightly compressed and wavy.
Smell is not distinctive.

COMMENTS
A very common and gregarious
species, often found in quite large
groups with other waxcaps in
unimproved grassland, usually
in late autumn.

KEY FACT
Another quite
variable species as regards size
and colour. It could be confused
with the similar Cedarwood
Waxcap *Hygrocybe russocoriacea*
but that species has a strong
smell of cedar.

SPOTTER'S CHART

LOCATION	DATE/TIME

PARROT WAXCAP
Hygrocybe psittacina

IDENTIFICATION

Cap is hemispherical to bell-shaped, gradually flattening; viscid and translucently striate; initially dark green, becoming more yellow-brown. Gills are adnate to sinuate; edge not viscid; concolourous with, or a shade paler than, cap. Stem is cylindrical, often irregularly compressed and wavy, viscid, green at top.

KEY FACT

A surprisingly tricky species to identify as the expected green colour of the fruit body is not always present, or sometimes confined to the stem apex. The Heath Waxcap *Hygrocybe laeta* is similar but has decurrent gills with a viscid edge.

COMMENTS

Grows gregariously and has a preference for unimproved grassland, but can be hard to spot owing to its green colour and small stature.

SPOTTER'S CHART

LOCATION	DATE/TIME

IVORY WOODWAX
Hygrophorus eburneus

FACT FILE

SIZE Cap diameter 2–7cm; height 3–12cm
HABITAT Mainly found under Beech STATUS Widespread
and occasional FRUITING SEASON Aug–Nov

IDENTIFICATION
Cap is hemispherical to broadly
bell-shaped, slimy when moist,
pure white. Gills are adnate to
slightly decurrent, broad, fairly
widely spaced, white. Stem is
cylindrical, tapering downwards,
with small cottony scales at apex
and smoother below, slimy when
moist, white. Smells pleasant and
distinctly sweet.

KEY FACT
The similar
Yellowing Woodwax *Hygrophorus
discoxanthus* discolours brownish
with age and usually occurs
under Beech on chalk, while
H. cossus discolours creamy
grey and is rare under oaks.

COMMENTS
Found singly or in small groups
in leaf-litter under Beech in the
autumn. Look out for the slimy,
sweet-smelling all-white fruit
bodies with decurrent gills.

SPOTTER'S CHART

LOCATION	DATE/TIME

FACT FILE

SIZE **Cap diameter 2–8cm; height 5–15cm**
HABITAT **Parasitic and saprotrophic on wood of deciduous trees**
STATUS **Widespread and very common** FRUITING SEASON **Aug–Oct**

IDENTIFICATION

Cap is rounded, expanding with age, finally flat to upturned at margin; olive-yellow with a browner centre that has many erect brown scales. Gills are adnate, medium-spaced. Stem is cylindrical, tapering, with a large membranous and persistent ring; cream, grading to browner below and covered in small whitish veil remnants.

KEY FACT

Causes an intense white rot in hardwood trees. Being saprotrophic as well as parasitic, it does not have to modify its growth to prevent killing the host tree and thus causes much damage in forests and gardens.

COMMENTS

Grows densely tufted on wood or at the base of trees. The blackish bootlace-like rhizomorphs that help it spread are often conspicuous on partly rotten trunks.

SPOTTER'S CHART

LOCATION	DATE/TIME

SULPHUR KNIGHT
Tricholoma sulphureum

FACT FILE

SIZE Cap diameter 2–7cm; height 3–10cm
HABITAT Mainly under oaks, less commonly under Beech
STATUS Widespread and very common FRUITING SEASON Aug–Nov

IDENTIFICATION

Cap is hemispherical, expanding and flattening; bright sulphur yellow. Gills are adnate, thick and widely spaced, yellow. Stem is cylindrical, fibrillose; sulphur yellow, becoming reddish brown with age. Flesh is bright sulphur yellow. Smell is strong, gas-like.

KEY FACT The species' most distinctive feature is its strong, unpleasant gas-like smell, which gave rise to its alternative English name of Gasworks Tricholoma. The similar Yellow Knight *Tricholoma equestre* lacks the strong smell.

COMMENTS

An all-yellow species typically fruiting in large groups in leaf-litter, especially beside paths and road verges where oaks are present.

SPOTTER'S CHART

LOCATION	DATE/TIME

YELLOWING KNIGHT
Tricholoma sculpturatum

FACT FILE

SIZE Cap diameter 3–6cm; height 3–8cm

HABITAT Deciduous woodland, especially under Beech and birches

STATUS Widespread and occasional FRUITING SEASON Sep–Oct

IDENTIFICATION

Cap is convex, flattening over time; light grey or light brown, sometimes darker towards centre and flecked with fine, dark-tipped scales. Gills are adnate to sinuate; white to pale grey, yellowing with age. Stem is cylindrical, smooth; whitish, often flushed with cap colour. Smells strongly mealy; tastes mild.

KEY FACT

A difficult species to identify owing to the existence of several similar species and the fact that the yellowing is usually present only in older specimens. The mild taste is a useful character, as some similar species are burning-hot.

COMMENTS

Usually found growing in groups, these sometimes quite large, and often with several fused together at the stem base.

SPOTTER'S CHART

LOCATION	DATE/TIME

BIRCH KNIGHT
Tricholoma fulvum

FACT FILE

SIZE **Cap diameter 3–10cm; height 3–10cm**
HABITAT **Mainly under birches on acidic soil** STATUS **Widespread
and common** FRUITING SEASON **Aug–Nov**

IDENTIFICATION
Cap is convex, flattening,
often with a low umbo;
surface is finely and radially
fibrillose; reddish brown with
a paler, distinctly ribbed
margin. Gills are sinuate;
pale yellow, spotting rust
with age. Stem is cylindrical,
pale at apex and streaked
with rusty fibrils on a white
to pale yellow ground below.

SPOTTER'S CHART

LOCATION	DATE/TIME

COMMENTS
Usually found growing close to
birches, with which it forms a
mycorrhizal partnership. It is
especially prevalent on acid soils
such as heathland.

KEY FACT

A species that
is not too difficult to identify if
the ribbed cap margin (most
evident in older specimens),
rust-spotted yellowish gills and
yellow stem flesh are all taken
into consideration.

FACT FILE

SIZE Cap diameter 4–10cm; height 3–8cm
HABITAT Grassy woodland edges, beside paths, meadows, gardens
STATUS Widespread and common **FRUITING SEASON** Apr–May

IDENTIFICATION

Cap is irregularly hemispherical to convex, with an inrolled, often wavy margin; white to cream. Gills are adnexed, often with a decurrent tooth; crowded; white to pale cream. Stem is stout and cylindrical, often with a bulbous base; concolourous with cap. Smells mealy.

KEY FACT

A good edible, though could be confused with some superficially similar but poisonous springtime species. One such is the Deadly Fibrecap *Inocybe erubescens*, which differs in that most parts stain red with age and on bruising.

SPOTTER'S CHART

LOCATION	DATE/TIME

COMMENTS

The species' common name refers to the peak time of year it fruits, that being St George's Day (23 Apr).

PLUMS AND CUSTARD
Tricholomopsis rutilans

FACT FILE

SIZE Cap diameter 3–12cm; height 3–10cm
HABITAT Stumps and rotting wood of conifers, especially pines
STATUS Widespread and common **FRUITING SEASON** Aug–Nov

IDENTIFICATION
Cap is convex, later flattening, often with an irregular margin; densely covered in purple red scales on a yellow ground, darker towards centre. Gills are adnate, crowded, yellow. Stem is often curved, densely covered in fine purple-red scales on a yellow ground.

KEY FACT Some specimens can be difficult to identify as the caps can vary markedly in colour, but the habit of growing on decaying conifer wood and the crowded yellow gills are good pointers.

COMMENTS
A distinctive and beautiful species typically encountered tightly clustered on rotting stumps of pine and, less commonly, spruce in late summer and autumn.

SPOTTER'S CHART

LOCATION	DATE/TIME

WHITELACED SHANK
Megacollybia platyphylla

FACT FILE

SIZE **Cap diameter 5–15cm; height 5–15cm**
HABITAT **Decayed and buried wood of deciduous trees**
STATUS **Widespread and common** FRUITING SEASON **Jun–Oct**

IDENTIFICATION
Cap is convex, flattening, distinctly radially fibrillose, often splitting with age; grey-brown, darker in centre. Gills are adnate, broad, widely spaced, white to cream. Stem is cylindrical, wider at base and with white rhizomorphs attached; fibrillose; off-white to grey-brown.

COMMENTS
A large species growing singly or, more often, in small groups in deciduous woodland in the autumn.

KEY FACT
The characteristic feature of this species, hinted at in its common name, is the white lace-like rhizomorphs attached to the stem base. Some careful excavating is required to reveal them.

SPOTTER'S CHART

LOCATION	DATE/TIME

CLOUDED FUNNEL
Clitocybe nebularis

FACT FILE

SIZE **Cap diameter 5–15cm; height 5–10cm**
HABITAT **Deciduous and coniferous woodland, gardens, parks**
STATUS **Widespread and very common** FRUITING SEASON **Oct–Dec**

IDENTIFICATION

Cap is convex, flattening, sometimes with a low, broad umbo or central depression, margin inrolled and sometimes wavy; smoky grey-brown, darker towards centre. Gills are decurrent, crowded, cream. Stem is cylindrical to swollen at base, fibrillose, white to pale grey-brown. Smells mealy.

KEY FACT An interesting and rare little fungus known as the Piggyback Rosegill *Volvariella surrecta* is parasitic on this species. It can sometimes be encountered growing on the caps, often causing the whole fruit body to be deformed.

COMMENTS

Usually starts appearing around mid-Oct, with many fruiting together in large rings or groups on the woodland floor.

SPOTTER'S CHART

LOCATION	DATE/TIME

SIZE Cap diameter 3–8cm; height 3–8cm
HABITAT Deciduous and, less commonly, coniferous woodland
STATUS Widespread and common **FRUITING SEASON** Aug–Nov

IDENTIFICATION

Cap is convex with a central depression, becoming more funnel-shaped and wavy-edged; pale pinkish buff. Gills are strongly decurrent, narrow, crowded. Stem is cylindrical, slightly wider towards base; paler than cap and often covered with white down at base.

COMMENTS

A good edible with a pleasant smell, appearing singly or, more often, in small groups on the ground among leaf-litter.

KEY FACT

Look out for the deeply funnelled, thin-fleshed caps of mature specimens, which sometimes develop a wavy edge. The caps often have a pink tinge and the gills run a long way down the stem.

SPOTTER'S CHART

LOCATION	DATE/TIME

ANISEED FUNNEL
Clitocybe odora

FACT FILE

SIZE Cap diameter 3–10cm; height 3–7cm
HABITAT Mainly deciduous woodland; less often with conifers
STATUS Widespread and common FRUITING SEASON Aug–Oct

IDENTIFICATION
Cap is convex with an inrolled
margin, becoming funnelled with
a wavy edge; surface is smooth,
greenish blue, varying in intensity
and fading greyish with age. Gills
are adnate to slightly decurrent,
crowded, concolourous with cap.
Stem is cylindrical, generally paler
than the cap, covered in white
down at the base. Smells strongly
of aniseed.

SPOTTER'S CHART

LOCATION	DATE/TIME

KEY FACT
A striking and
easily identified species when
fresh, on account of its smell
and greenish-blue colours. Older
specimens may fade but still
retain the strong aniseed smell,
when they may be mistaken for
the smaller Fragrant Funnel
Clitocybe fragrans.

COMMENTS
A strong aniseed scent in the air
is often the first indication that
this species is in the vicinity.

FACT FILE

SIZE **Cap diameter 3–8cm; height 5–12cm**
HABITAT **Deciduous and coniferous woodland** STATUS **Widespread and common** FRUITING SEASON **Oct–Jan**

IDENTIFICATION

Cap is funnel-shaped with an inrolled margin; colour varies considerably between specimens, from pale brown to dark brown and usually darker towards centre. Gills are decurrent, forking, whitish. Stem is cylindrical, thicker towards base; covered in brown longitudinal fibres and white down at base.

KEY FACT A distinctive species with forking gills, the presence of which helps separate it from the funnel caps. The very similar *Pseudoclitocybe expallens* is smaller and very rare.

COMMENTS

Usually starts fruiting late in the autumn, when it occurs singly or in small groups in soil or, occasionally, on very rotten wood.

SPOTTER'S CHART

LOCATION	DATE/TIME

VELVET SHANK
Flammulina velutipes

FACT FILE

SIZE Cap diameter 2–6cm; height 2–6cm
HABITAT On dead or dying wood of deciduous trees
STATUS Widespread and very common FRUITING SEASON Nov–Feb

IDENTIFICATION
Cap is hemispherical with a striate margin, slimy when wet; orange overall, reddish brown towards centre, yellow towards margin. Gills are adnate to sinuate, medium-crowded, pale creamy buff. Stem is cylindrical, often curved, tough and covered in dark brown velvety hairs.

SPOTTER'S CHART

LOCATION	DATE/TIME

KEY FACT
Fruiting time, clustered growth habit on stumps and other dead wood, a slimy, bright orange cap and a velvety stem are all characters that help identify this common winter species.

COMMENTS
A winter fruiting species typically found growing on stumps of deciduous trees such as elms and sycamores. It is also common on stumps and wound sites of Common Gorse on heathland.

FACT FILE

SIZE Cap diameter 1–4cm; height 3–8cm
HABITAT Deciduous and coniferous woodland, heathland, gardens
STATUS Widespread and very common **FRUITING SEASON** Jul–Nov

IDENTIFICATION

Cap is hemispherical, later flattening, sometimes with a small depression in centre; margin is striate; surface is often scurfy, pale buff to deep orange-rust. Gills are adnate to shortly decurrent, widely spaced, pale pinkish buff. Stem is cylindrical, fibrous, sometimes twisted and often darker than cap.

COMMENTS

Only the caps are edible as the stems are too tough. Overall, The Deceiver is best avoided owing to possible confusion with some very poisonous species.

KEY FACT

The Deceiver is an apt name as the cap is strongly hygrophanous, meaning it changes colour considerably on drying. In this species, the colour changes from deep orange when wet to very pale buff when dry.

SPOTTER'S CHART

LOCATION	DATE/TIME

AMETHYST DECEIVER
Laccaria amethystina

FACT FILE

SIZE Cap diameter 3–7cm; height 3–10cm
HABITAT Associated with various deciduous trees
STATUS Widespread and very common **FRUITING SEASON** Aug–Nov

IDENTIFICATION
Cap is hemispherical, later flattening, sometimes with a small depression in centre; margin is striate; surface is often scurfy, pale grey to deep violet. Gills are adnate to shortly decurrent, widely spaced. Stem is cylindrical, fibrous, sometimes twisted and often darker than cap.

COMMENTS
Forms a mycorrhizal partnership with the roots of various deciduous trees, including Beech and birches, sometimes fruiting abundantly beneath them.

KEY FACT
Very similar to The Deceiver and once thought to be just a variety of that species. It differs most obviously in the colour of the fruit bodies, which are violet when wet and almost white when dry.

SPOTTER'S CHART

LOCATION	DATE/TIME

FACT FILE

SIZE Cap diameter 3–8cm; height 5–10cm
HABITAT Parasitic on roots of oak trees STATUS Widespread and
common in the S, rare in the N FRUITING SEASON Jul–Oct

IDENTIFICATION

Cap is convex, sometimes
flattening or becoming
misshapen; surface is
smooth; light to deep
red-brown, often streaked
or spotted darker. Gills are
widely spaced; buff, spotted
red-brown with age. Stem
is tough and fibrous, long,
contorted and grooved,
rooting and fusing with
others at base.

COMMENTS

Stems are very tough, with
many fusing together at the base
to form tight clusters at the foot
of mature oak trees from
midsummer onwards.

KEY FACT Causes root
rot in mature oak trees that
can be quite extensive. This,
in turn, leads to a slow-down
and deterioration in the tree's
development, sometimes visible
as a dying back of the crown.

SPOTTER'S CHART

LOCATION	DATE/TIME

WOOD WOOLLYFOOT
Collybia peronata

FACT FILE

SIZE **Cap diameter 3–7cm; height 3–8cm**
HABITAT **Leaf-litter of deciduous trees, rarely conifers**
STATUS **Widespread and common** FRUITING SEASON **Sep–Nov**

IDENTIFICATION
Cap is convex, flattening and becoming wrinkled with a texture akin to chamois leather; pale orange-brown with a pale yellow margin. Gills are adnexed to free, narrow, widely spaced, pale yellow-brown. Stem is cylindrical, tough, pale yellowish, base densely covered in yellowish hairs.

KEY FACT The caps of this species are quite distinctive once known, but the best characters for identification are probably the tough stem, which can be twisted without breaking, and the densely yellow-haired stem base.

COMMENTS
Typically found growing in small scattered groups in the leaf-litter of deciduous trees, especially Beech, in autumn.

SPOTTER'S CHART

LOCATION	DATE/TIME

SPOTTED TOUGHSHANK
Collybia maculata

FACT FILE SIZE **Cap diameter 4–10cm; height 5–12cm**
HABITAT **In needle-litter in conifer woodland** STATUS **Widespread and common** FRUITING SEASON **Aug–Nov**

IDENTIFICATION
Cap is convex, smooth; white at first, later developing rusty spots. Gills are sinuate, narrow, crowded, white but developing rusty spots with age. Stem is tough, fibrous, tapering, sometimes rooting; white with rusty spots, especially near base. Spore deposit is cream with a pinkish tinge.

SPOTTER'S CHART

LOCATION	DATE/TIME

COMMENTS
A tough, bitter-tasting, inedible species that typically grows in groups in pine-needle litter, sometimes abundantly.

KEY FACT
Also known as Foxy Spots on account of the rusty spotting. It differs from some other *Collybia* species in that it has a pinkish tinge to the spore deposit, although this can be hard to detect unless a fairly thick layer is obtained.

BUTTER CAP
Collybia butyracea

FACT FILE

SIZE Cap diameter 3–8cm; height 5–10cm
HABITAT Soil and leaf-litter in deciduous and coniferous woodland
STATUS Widespread and very common FRUITING SEASON Sep–Jan

IDENTIFICATION
Cap is convex, flattening and sometimes becoming upturned at margin; smooth and greasy; colour is extremely variable, from pale grey to dark brown and often zoned. Gills are adnexed to free, white. Stem is tough, fibrous and hollow, swollen at base, reddish brown or concolourous with cap.

KEY FACT Once familiarity with the look and feel of the greasy or buttery cap is acquired, this becomes a fairly straightforward species to identify despite the huge range of its colour forms.

COMMENTS
One of the commonest and most abundant species occurring in woodlands throughout the British Isles in autumn and early winter.

SPOTTER'S CHART

LOCATION	DATE/TIME

FAIRY RING CHAMPIGNON
Marasmius oreades

SIZE **Cap diameter 2–5cm; height 3–8cm**

HABITAT **Grassland, including meadows, dunes, lawns and parks**

STATUS **Widespread and very common** FRUITING SEASON **Jun–Oct**

IDENTIFICATION
Cap is bell-shaped, flattening with a low, broad umbo; surface smooth, tan with a paler margin, whole cap drying paler. Gills are free, medium-spaced, pale creamy buff. Stem is cylindrical, tough and solid, not snapping when twisted, light buff. Smells pleasantly of bitter almonds.

KEY FACT The fairy ring effect is visible even when the fungus is not fruiting, as there is usually a ring of darker green nutrient-rich grass enclosing a lighter, nutrient-depleted centre.

COMMENTS
Famous for forming 'fairy rings' in grassland, which can reach well over 10m across after many years of expanding growth.

SPOTTER'S CHART

LOCATION	DATE/TIME

COLLARED PARACHUTE
Marasmius rotula

FACT FILE

SIZE Cap diameter 0.5–2cm; height 2–6cm
HABITAT On buried or exposed twigs of deciduous trees
STATUS Widespread and very common FRUITING SEASON Jul–Nov

IDENTIFICATION
Cap is convex with a central depression, radially furrowed, ivory white with a darker navel. Gills are distant, not connected to stem directly but cogwheel-like to a small collar encircling it; white to cream. Stem is tough and wiry, reminiscent of horsehair; dark brown to black.

COMMENTS
Typically found in small clusters on the buried twigs of broadleaved trees in deciduous woodland, especially after heavy rain in late summer to early autumn.

KEY FACT

This and other species of *Marasmius* are remarkable for their ability to survive multiple cycles of desiccation. Once revived with sufficient moisture, the gills can even start producing spores again.

SPOTTER'S CHART

LOCATION	DATE/TIME

SIZE **Cap diameter 0.5–2cm; height 0.5–2cm**
HABITAT **Twigs of various trees, dead stems of Bramble**
STATUS **Widespread and common** FRUITING SEASON **Jul–Dec**

IDENTIFICATION
Cap is convex, flattening and becoming more undulating and wrinkled with age; cream to pale tan. Gills are adnate, attaching directly to stem and not to a collar; widely spaced; cream to beige. Stem is short, curved and beige, with small, pale cottony scales at base.

KEY FACT This species is quite different from the Collared Parachute in that the gills attach directly to the stem rather than to a collar. The stem itself is not black or horsehair-like as in many other parachutes.

COMMENTS
Usually found fruiting in dense clusters along the fallen twigs of various trees such as the Common Larch but also, and perhaps most commonly, along dead stems of Brambles.

SPOTTER'S CHART

LOCATION	DATE/TIME

ROOTING SHANK
Xerula radicata

FACT FILE

SIZE **Cap diameter 3–10cm; height 5–20cm**
HABITAT **On buried wood in deciduous woodland**
STATUS **Widespread and very common** FRUITING SEASON **Jul–Nov**

IDENTIFICATION
Cap is convex, flattening and becoming somewhat upturned at margin, with a central umbo; surface is smooth, slimy when moist, radially wrinkled, grey-brown to yellow-brown. Gills are adnate with a decurrent tooth, widely spaced, white but developing a brown edge. Stem is long and slender, tapering upwards, deeply rooting.

KEY FACT A significant feature of this species is the very long rooting stem, which attaches to buried wood. Fortunately, there is no need to dig up each individual to confirm this, as the aerial portion is quite distinctive.

COMMENTS
Commonly found from late summer onwards, usually singly or in small groups on the ground in deciduous woods.

SPOTTER'S CHART	
LOCATION	DATE/TIME

FACT FILE SIZE Cap diameter 4–8cm; height 4–8cm HABITAT In humus and leaf-litter in deciduous and coniferous woodland STATUS Widespread and very common FRUITING SEASON Sep–Dec

IDENTIFICATION
Cap is initially convex with a central depression and inrolled margin, gradually becoming more funnel-shaped; pale buff to deep orange-brown, sometimes developing rusty spots. Gills are deeply decurrent, crowded, cream to pale brown and normally paler than cap. Stem is cylindrical, smooth to fibrillose.

KEY FACT Could be confused with the Common Funnel, but that species is usually smaller and more slender, and doesn't grow in such large, dense groups.

COMMENTS
A very common species, typically found growing in dense rings or troops on compost heaps or deep leaf-litter in late autumn.

SPOTTER'S CHART

LOCATION	DATE/TIME

WOOD BLEWIT
Lepista nuda

SIZE Cap diameter 5–15cm; height 5–10cm
HABITAT In leaf-litter and compost in woods, parks and gardens
STATUS Widespread and very common **FRUITING SEASON** Sep–Dec

IDENTIFICATION

Cap is convex with an inrolled margin; surface is smooth, deep lilac to pinkish brown. Gills are adnate, medium-spaced, lilac but becoming paler and browner with age. Stem is cylindrical, fairly stout, fibrillose, greyish lilac. Smells strongly aromatic.

COMMENTS

A good edible that can be found growing in troops in the garden, especially on compost heaps and piles of decaying leaf-litter.

KEY FACT

A robust species that is fairly easy to recognise in the field but can be confused with the related but more slender *Lepista sordida*, which grows in similar habitats.

SPOTTER'S CHART

LOCATION	DATE/TIME

PORCELAIN FUNGUS
Oudemansiella mucida

FACT FILE

SIZE **Cap diameter 2–8cm; height 2–10cm**
HABITAT **On fallen or attached branches of Beech**
STATUS **Widespread and common** FRUITING SEASON **Aug–Dec**

KEY FACT

Easily recognised by its clustered growth habit on
Beech branches, and its slimy, translucent white caps and persistent
ring. No other white fungus in Britain has this suite of characters.

IDENTIFICATION

Cap is hemispherical to convex; smooth and slimy; translucently white,
though sometimes with brown tones and often a shade darker towards
centre. Gills are widely spaced,
white. Stem is cylindrical and
curving, thicker at base;
grooved above persistent ring,
which is membranous and
often upturned.

COMMENTS

The almost exclusive habitat
of this species is branches of
Beech trees, either still
attached or on the ground.

SPOTTER'S CHART

LOCATION	DATE/TIME

CONIFERCONE CAP
Baeospora myosura

SIZE Cap diameter 1–2cm; height 2–7cm
HABITAT On partially buried cones of conifers, especially pines
STATUS Widespread and common **FRUITING SEASON** Sep–Jan

IDENTIFICATION
Cap is convex at first, later flattening, usually with a small central umbo; tan, paling towards margin. Gills are very crowded, narrow, pale beige. Stem is cylindrical, straight, hollow, covered in a powdery bloom when fresh, paler than cap.

KEY FACT
There are several other cone-inhabiting species but this is by far the commonest in autumn. The very crowded gills and pale, powdery stem help distinguish it from most look-alikes.

COMMENTS
Although small, this species fruits gregariously – a single cone can harbour many fruiting bodies, making them a little easier to spot on the woodland floor.

SPOTTER'S CHART

LOCATION	DATE/TIME

FACT FILE

SIZE **Cap diameter 2–5cm; height 5–15cm**

HABITAT **On decayed wood of deciduous trees, often partially buried**

STATUS **Widespread and common** FRUITING SEASON **Aug–Dec**

IDENTIFICATION

Cap is initially conical, expanding and flattening with a prominent central umbo, and finally with an upturned margin; surface is radially grooved, dark greyish brown to pale grey. Gills are pale grey. Stem is tall and straight, longitudinally grooved and twisted, rooting, greyish.

COMMENTS

Grows singly or with several others close together on fallen branches or buried wood of deciduous trees, and shows a preference for oaks and Hazel.

KEY FACT

The best feature for identifying the species in the field is its longitudinally grooved stem, which also has a tendency to twist as it grows.

SPOTTER'S CHART

LOCATION	DATE/TIME

COMMON BONNET
Mycena galericulata

FACT FILE

SIZE **Cap diameter 3–6cm; height 5–10 cm**
HABITAT **On decayed logs and stumps in deciduous woodland**
STATUS **Widespread and very common** FRUITING SEASON **Jul–Nov**

IDENTIFICATION
Cap is bell-shaped, flattening with a central umbo; surface is often grooved or wrinkled, greyish brown to tan, with a lighter margin and darker centre. Gills are adnexed, finely inter-veined at their base; whitish, becoming pinkish. Stem is very tough, elastic, hollow; dark brown, becoming pale grey.

COMMENTS
Typically encountered in dense clusters on fallen trunks, logs and stumps in deciduous woodland in autumn.

KEY FACT
The specific epithet *galericulata* is derived from the galleries formed by the many fine, interconnecting veins present at the base of the gills where they connect with the cap.

SPOTTER'S CHART

LOCATION	DATE/TIME

FACT FILE

SIZE **Cap diameter 0.5–2cm; height 3–6cm**
HABITAT **Mainly on the ground in deciduous and coniferous woodland**
STATUS **Widespread and common** FRUITING SEASON **Aug–Dec**

IDENTIFICATION

Cap is hemispherical to conical, radially striate; extremely variable in colour, from white through shades of brown to almost black. Gills are adnexed, distant, whitish. Stem is smooth to slightly pubescent, variably coloured but usually darker towards base, and contains copious white milky fluid.

COMMENTS

Grows in scattered groups or with several together in a wide range of habitats, from woody debris and leaf-litter to lawns and burnt heathland.

KEY FACT

The characteristic feature of this species is the copious milky fluid present in the stem, especially near the base, revealed when it is snapped. Note also that the gills are quite widely spaced for a bonnet.

SPOTTER'S CHART

LOCATION	DATE/TIME

BURGUNDYDROP BONNET
Mycena haematopus

FACT FILE

SIZE **Cap diameter 1–3cm; height 3–7cm**
HABITAT **On decayed wood of deciduous trees**
STATUS **Widespread and common** FRUITING SEASON **Aug–Nov**

IDENTIFICATION
Cap is bell-shaped, striate, covered in fine white powder; margin is scalloped; dark reddish brown in centre, lighter towards margin, drying pale pinkish. Gills are adnexed; whitish, becoming tinged reddish brown. Stem is brittle, curved, initially covered in dense, fine powder; exudes blood-red fluid when broken.

KEY FACT The species' tufted growth habit on decaying wood, together with the blood-red liquid exuded from the stem when it is broken, are good characters separating it from similar relatives.

COMMENTS
Typically encountered growing tufted, with all stems arising from a common base, on decaying trunks, branches and stumps of deciduous trees.

SPOTTER'S CHART

LOCATION	DATE/TIME

SIZE **Cap diameter 3–6cm; height 5–10cm**
HABITAT **In deciduous woodland especially Beech**
STATUS **Widespread and common** FRUITING SEASON **Aug–Dec**

IDENTIFICATION
Cap is convex, flattening, often with a low umbo, striate, varying in colour from almost white to rosy pink. Gills are sinuate, fairly crowded, white to pale pink. Stem is cylindrical, hollow, white and sometimes with a hint of pink. Smells of radishes.

KEY FACT
Some people consider this species as being merely a robust pink variety of the Lilac Bonnet *Mycena pura*. However, the Lilac Bonnet is smaller and has lilac rather than pink tones in the cap and stem. Both species are poisonous.

SPOTTER'S CHART

LOCATION	DATE/TIME

COMMENTS
A species typically encountered fruiting in leaf litter under Beech trees in the autumn. It appears to be quite common in S England but scarcer further N.

BLACKEDGE BONNET
Mycena pelianthina

FACT FILE

SIZE **Cap diameter 3–6cm; height 3–7cm**
HABITAT **Leaf-litter of Beech trees** STATUS **Widespread,
though common only in S England** FRUITING SEASON **Sep–Nov**

IDENTIFICATION

Cap is convex, flattening; lilac-brown when young, later pale greyish lilac
and often paler in centre with a darker marginal zone as it dries; margin
striate. Gills are sinuate; lilac,
greying with a dark edge. Stem is
cylindrical, hollow, fibrillose, usually
fairly pale greyish lilac. Smells
strongly of radishes.

COMMENTS

Grows singly or in small groups in
damp leaf-litter under Beech trees
in the autumn.

KEY FACT

The dark edge
to the gills is the best character
in helping distinguish this from
similar species growing in Beech
litter, such as Rosy Bonnet and
Lilac Bonnet *Mycena pura*.

SPOTTER'S CHART

LOCATION	DATE/TIME

FACT FILE

SIZE **Cap diameter 1–3cm; height 3–10cm**
HABITAT **Mainly on decayed wood of oak** STATUS **Widespread and very common** FRUITING SEASON **Sep–Dec**

IDENTIFICATION

Cap is conical to bell-shaped, with radial striations and a scalloped margin; pale buff to reddish brown. Gills are adnexed to adnate with a decurrent tooth, crowded; white, discolouring pinkish. Stem is long and slender, curving; white at top, then yellowish grading to dark reddish brown towards base. Smells spicy.

KEY FACT The stem of this species is quite distinctive and usually more consistent than the cap, although the scalloped cap margin is a useful character.

COMMENTS

Typically encountered growing in dense tufts on stumps, branches and other wood of oaks and, sometimes, Sweet Chestnut in the autumn.

SPOTTER'S CHART

LOCATION	DATE/TIME

YELLOWLEG BONNET
Mycena epipterygia

SIZE **Cap diameter 0.5–2cm; height 3–7cm**
HABITAT **Mainly on needle-litter and woody debris under conifers**
STATUS **Widespread and common** FRUITING SEASON **Sep–Dec**

KEY FACT
The species' main feature is the detachable elastic layer on the cap, stem and gill edge. This, combined with the lemon-yellow stem, should help identify it.

IDENTIFICATION
Cap is egg-shaped, expanding to bell-shaped or convex with a small umbo; striate, viscid, outer layer elastic and detachable; colour is variable but mainly greyish to yellowish brown. Gills are whitish, edge detachable as an elastic thread. Stem is slender, slimy, pale to bright lemon yellow.

COMMENTS
A widely occurring species, most commonly encountered growing in troops on needle-litter or decaying woody debris of conifers in the autumn.

SPOTTER'S CHART

LOCATION	DATE/TIME

FACT FILE

SIZE Cap diameter 0.5–1.5cm; height 1–4cm
HABITAT On soil in grassland and moss in woods, heaths and gardens
STATUS Widespread and very common **FRUITING SEASON** Jul–Dec

IDENTIFICATION

Cap is hemispherical, flattening with a depressed centre like a navel; margin is striate and edge sometimes scalloped; bright orange, darker in centre. Gills are deeply decurrent, distant, whitish. Stem is slender, wavy, hollow, finely hairy, pale orange.

KEY FACT A beautiful and distinctive species not likely to be confused with anything else. The closely related Collared Mosscap *Rickenella swartzii* often grows nearby but its cap is very pale brown with a dark brown centre.

COMMENTS

A very small but conspicuous species commonly found growing singly or scattered on lawns and playing fields, and among moss in woodland and heaths.

SPOTTER'S CHART

LOCATION	DATE/TIME

BITTER OYSTERLING
Panellus stipticus

FACT FILE

SIZE Cap diameter 1–3cm; stem length 0.5–2cm
HABITAT On wood of deciduous trees, especially oaks
STATUS Widespread and very common FRUITING SEASON Sep–Jan

IDENTIFICATION
Cap is convex, shell-shaped; margin is inrolled at first, edge becoming wavy or even scalloped; surface is velvety to scurfy, later sometimes finely cracked, cream to tan. Gills are crowded, often forked and with interconnecting veins, cream to tan. Stem is eccentric, short, finely hairy, cream.

KEY FACT The species is said to be bioluminescent, especially the gills, although this may not easily be observed in the wild if conditions are not dark enough and as the effect is fairly weak.

COMMENTS
A very common species, especially in winter, when it is typically found fruiting in dense, overlapping tiers on stumps and fallen branches of oaks.

SPOTTER'S CHART

LOCATION	DATE/TIME

FACT FILE

SIZE **Cap diameter 3–10cm; height 2–6cm**
HABITAT **Mainly on decaying trunks and logs of elms**
STATUS **Widespread and occasional** FRUITING SEASON **Sep–Nov**

KEY FACT

The appearance of the cap can be quite variable.
Initially, the gelatinous surface gives rise to interconnecting ridges that can form a network or give a wrinkled appearance. Over time, this layer breaks down and can appear as a slimy coating.

IDENTIFICATION

Cap is convex with a deeply inrolled margin, expanding and flattening; surface is gelatinous, apricot, with or without a raised white network, dry or slimy and often exuding reddish droplets. Gills are white to pale salmon. Stem is fairly short and curved, often eccentric; white, sometimes with reddish droplets.

SPOTTER'S CHART

LOCATION	DATE/TIME

COMMENTS

A beautiful and distinctive species, found almost exclusively on decaying elm wood that has recently had a good soaking.

LIVID PINKGILL
Entoloma sinuatum

FACT FILE

SIZE Cap diameter 5–20cm; height 5–15cm
HABITAT On the ground in deciduous woodland, especially oak and
Beech STATUS Widespread and scarce FRUITING SEASON Aug–Oct

IDENTIFICATION
Cap is convex, expanding, sometimes with a low, broad umbo and wavy
edge; flesh is thick; surface is dry and smooth, light grey-brown. Gills are
sinuate, medium-spaced, pale creamy buff. Stem is stout, cylindrical,
white to greyish. Spore deposit is pale salmon pink.

COMMENTS
The New Forest is a
stronghold for this
otherwise scarce
species. It is best looked
for in late summer to
early autumn under
oaks or Beech.

KEY FACT

An alternative name for
this species is Lead Poisoner – it has
accounted for numerous poisonings,
causing mainly gastro-intestinal upsets.
Note the sinuate, not decurrent, gills and
salmon-pink spore deposit.

SPOTTER'S CHART

LOCATION	DATE/TIME

FACT FILE

SIZE Cap diameter 3–10cm; height 2–6cm
HABITAT In open grassy areas near deciduous trees
STATUS Widespread and very common FRUITING SEASON Aug–Oct

IDENTIFICATION

Cap is convex; margin is inrolled for some time, edge becoming irregularly wavy or lobed; surface texture is suede-like, greyish white. Gills are distinctly decurrent; white, then pink. Stem is cylindrical, smooth, often eccentric and curving, concolourous with cap. Spore deposit is pink.

COMMENTS

Sometimes found growing singly, but more often in close groups and sometimes with multiple fruit bodies arising from a common base.

SPOTTER'S CHART

LOCATION	DATE/TIME

KEY FACT

Although edible, The Miller is best avoided as it is easily confused with similar but poisonous species, such as the white-spored and deadly Fool's Funnel *Clitocybe rivulosa*. The Livid Pinkgill is much more robust and does not have decurrent gills.

DEER SHIELD
Pluteus cervinus

FACT FILE

SIZE Cap diameter 4–15cm; height 4–12cm
HABITAT On decaying wood of deciduous trees including woodchips
STATUS Widespread and very common **FRUITING SEASON** Jun–Dec

IDENTIFICATION
Cap is initially somewhat irregularly egg-shaped, often with a bumpy surface, later convex to planar, with the bumps mostly smoothed out; fibrillose and scaly at centre, medium to dark brown. Gills are free, crowded, broad; white, then pink. Stem is cylindrical with brown fibrils on a white ground. Smells of radish.

COMMENTS
Very common on rotting logs and stumps of broadleaved trees, and increasingly so on woodchips, from summer through autumn.

> **KEY FACT**
>
> Although this species has been recorded on rotting conifer wood it is a rare occurrence; such finds are more likely to be the closely related *Pluteus pouzarianus* or *P. atromarginatus*, both of which are confined to this substrate.

SPOTTER'S CHART

LOCATION	DATE/TIME

FACT FILE SIZE Cap diameter 1.5–4cm; height 2–5 cm
HABITAT On decaying wood of deciduous trees STATUS Widespread and frequent in the S, rare further N FRUITING SEASON Aug–Dec

IDENTIFICATION
Cap is initially conical, expanding and flattening with a small umbo; smooth to finely wrinkled, especially in centre; brown when very young, then greenish to golden yellow, sometimes retaining a hint of brown. Gills are free, crowded; white, then pink. Stem is cylindrical; white to cream, yellowish at base.

COMMENTS
Frequently found growing singly or in small groups on very rotten wood of deciduous trees, such as elms, Beech and Ash, in autumn and early winter.

KEY FACT
Very similar in appearance to the Lion Shield *Pluteus leoninus,* and only reliably distinguished by microscopic examination of the structure of the cap surface. The Lion Shield also tends to be slightly bigger with a yellower stem.

SPOTTER'S CHART

LOCATION	DATE/TIME

STUBBLE ROSEGILL
Volvariella gloiocephala

FACT FILE

SIZE **Cap diameter 5–15cm; height 10–20cm**
HABITAT **Stubble fields, road verges, woodchips, mulch beds**
STATUS **Widespread and common** FRUITING SEASON **Aug–Dec**

KEY FACT Although an edible species, the Stubble Rosegill is best avoided as the presence of the volval bag might cause confusion with some of the deadly *Amanita* species. However, those species have white gills instead of pink and prefer a more wooded habitat.

IDENTIFICATION
Cap is initially bluntly conical, expanding and becoming convex to flat; smooth, greasy to viscid when moist; ivory white to greyish brown. Gills are free and crowded; white, then pink. Stem is cylindrical, tapering upwards; base is enclosed by a whitish volval bag.

SPOTTER'S CHART

LOCATION	DATE/TIME

COMMENTS
This species is now most often encountered growing on woodchips and mulch. However, it can still be prolific in some stubble fields.

FACT FILE

SIZE Cap diameter 1–3cm; height 4–8cm
HABITAT On the ground in deciduous woodland STATUS Widespread
and common FRUITING SEASON Aug–Nov

IDENTIFICATION

Cap is conical to convex
with a pointed umbo;
brown and covered in
white-tipped scales,
especially at margin.
Gills are greyish violet,
browning with age.
Stem is rigid, brown;
initially covered in a
silky white veil, which
gradually breaks up to
form a number of white
bands. Smells strongly
of pelargoniums.

COMMENTS

Commonly found growing in close
groups on the edge of paths in
deciduous woodland from late
summer into autumn.

KEY FACT

The species
has several very similar-looking
relatives, making identification
tricky. Fortunately, none of
them has the same strong
pelargonium smell.

SPOTTER'S CHART

LOCATION	DATE/TIME

RED BANDED WEBCAP
Cortinarius armillatus

FACT FILE

SIZE Cap diameter 5–12cm; height 8–15cm
HABITAT On the ground under birch and pine trees
STATUS Widespread and occasional FRUITING SEASON Sep–Oct

IDENTIFICATION

Cap is hemispherical and convex, with a low, broad umbo; orange-brown, covered in darker fine scales. Gills are adnate, medium-spaced; light brown, becoming darker rusty brown with age. Stem is tall, swollen at base, silkily fibrillose with several red bands.

KEY FACT A beautiful and distinctive species on account of the red banding on the stem, formed from the remnants of the universal veil that enveloped the whole fruit body when young.

COMMENTS

Typically encountered growing singly or in small groups on the ground where both birches and pines are present.

SPOTTER'S CHART

LOCATION	DATE/TIME

FACT FILE

SIZE Cap diameter 3–8cm; height 5–12cm
HABITAT On the ground in deciduous woodland STATUS Widespread and common FRUITING SEASON Aug–Nov

IDENTIFICATION

Cap is hemispherical to convex with a low, broad umbo; dry; pale ochre-brown with a lilaceous tint near margin when young. Gills are adnate, crowded; greyish lilac, becoming buff. Stem is cylindrical, base slightly swollen, fibrillose; white with lilaceous tints at apex and subtle silky bands below. Spore deposit is rusty brown.

KEY FACT

As its common name suggests, this species is quite variable; it may in fact be a 'species complex', meaning that more than one species is involved, although no one has yet managed to separate them reliably.

COMMENTS

Usually encountered singly or in small groups on the ground in or at the edge of deciduous woodland, especially birch.

SPOTTER'S CHART

LOCATION	DATE/TIME

BIRCH WEBCAP
Cortinarius triumphans

FACT FILE

SIZE Cap diameter 5–12cm; height 6–12cm
HABITAT On the ground, mainly with birch trees
STATUS Widespread and occasional FRUITING SEASON Sep–Oct

IDENTIFICATION
Cap is hemispherical to convex; surface is greasy with remnants of veil sometimes present, orange-yellow. Gills are adnate; grey-lilac, becoming rust-stained from spores. Stem is stout, pointed at base and covered in yellow girdles from cobweb-like veil, which becomes rust-stained from spores. Smell none or very faint.

COMMENTS
Occasionally found fruiting singly or in small groups close to birch trees, with which it forms a mycorrhizal partnership.

SPOTTER'S CHART

LOCATION	DATE/TIME

KEY FACT

The yellow to rust veil girdles on the stem, lack of violaceous tones in the cap margin and unchanging flesh colour when cut or bruised help to distinguish this species from similar relatives.

FACT FILE

SIZE Cap diameter 3–7cm; height 3–7cm

HABITAT Acid soil in deciduous woodland, especially Beech and oak

STATUS Widespread and occasional FRUITING SEASON Aug–Nov

IDENTIFICATION

Cap is hemispherical, expanding and becoming convex to flat, densely covered in bright rusty red scales on a white to pale yellow ground. Gills are adnate, medium-spaced; buff, then more rusty brown with age. Stem has rusty red bands on a pale ground, bruising yellow. Flesh is white, turning yellow when cut.

COMMENTS

Normally found growing in small groups on the ground, mainly under Beech, oaks and birches on acidic soils in the autumn.

KEY FACT

This is a striking species and easy to recognise in the field on account of its bright rusty red cap scales and stem bands. The yellow bruising of the stem is another good characteristic that can be tested for. It is poisonous.

SPOTTER'S CHART

LOCATION	DATE/TIME

BLOODRED WEBCAP
Cortinarius sanguineus

FACT FILE

SIZE Cap diameter 2–5cm; height 3–10cm
HABITAT Mainly coniferous woodland on acidic soil
STATUS Widespread and occasional FRUITING SEASON Sep–Nov

IDENTIFICATION
Cap is convex, sometimes with an umbo, sometimes with a central depression; surface is radially fibrillose, deep blood red. Gills are adnate; blood red, then tinged rusty from spores. Stem is cylindrical, often curving, fibrillose; concolourous with cap, later sometimes with rusty dusting from spores caught in the cobweb-like cortina.

KEY FACT
As in all webcaps, this species has a cobweb-like universal veil known as a cortina. This is best detected at the top of the stem just below the gills, where it becomes dusted rusty with the spores.

COMMENTS
A striking species, typically found growing singly or in small groups, often with moss and in association with conifers on acidic soil in the autumn.

SPOTTER'S CHART

LOCATION	DATE/TIME

SIZE Cap diameter 4–15cm; height 4–10cm
HABITAT On the ground in association with many deciduous trees
STATUS Widespread and common **FRUITING SEASON** Aug–Dec

IDENTIFICATION

Cap is convex at first with a tightly inrolled margin, later expanding and becoming centrally depressed to funnel-shaped; margin is downy; surface is yellowish brown, slimy when wet. Gills are strongly decurrent; yellowish, bruising dark brown. Stem is cylindrical, short and thick; concolourous with cap, bruising dark brown.

COMMENTS

A very common species found growing singly or in groups in partnership with a number of deciduous trees, especially birches, in the autumn.

KEY FACT
Despite being consumed in some countries, *Paxillus* species are considered poisonous, their effects being cumulative and potentially fatal. The dark brown bruising of the gills and stem should be tested for to aid identification.

SPOTTER'S CHART

LOCATION	DATE/TIME

COMMON RUSTGILL
Gymnopilus penetrans

FACT FILE

SIZE Cap diameter 3–8cm; height 3–8cm
HABITAT On rotting wood of conifers **STATUS** Widespread
and common **FRUITING SEASON** Jul–Dec

IDENTIFICATION
Cap is hemispherical
to convex, smooth to
finely fibrillose; rusty
orange, with a more
yellow margin. Gills
are adnate, crowded;
pale yellow, developing
ever more rusty brown
spots with age. Stem is
cylindrical; pale yellow,
developing rusty brown
areas, base often with
white down.

KEY FACT
The much
scarcer Scaly Rustgill *Gymnopilus
sapineus* looks alike and grows
in similar habitats, but as its
common name suggests, it has
a scaly rather than fibrillose cap.

COMMENTS
Very common and sometimes
found in large numbers on woody
debris under conifer trees in
the autumn.

SPOTTER'S CHART

LOCATION	DATE/TIME

FACT FILE

SIZE **Cap diameter 3–10cm; height 3–8cm**
HABITAT **Mainly in mixed deciduous woodland**
STATUS **Widespread and common** FRUITING SEASON **Aug–Dec**

IDENTIFICATION

Cap is convex, flattening; margin is inrolled; surface is smooth, slimy when wet, white to cream, buff towards centre. Gills are sinuate, very crowded, exuding tiny clear droplets; pale brown, with darker brown spots as droplets dry. Stem is white, scurfy nearer apex. Smells of radish.

KEY FACT   As its common name suggests, this (as with all *Hebeloma* species) is considered to be poisonous. The radish-like smell is a useful characteristic, as are the very small droplets on the gill edges.

COMMENTS

Typically found growing in groups or rings in grass beside paths in deciduous woods, and forming a mycorrhizal partnership with some of those trees present.

SPOTTER'S CHART

LOCATION	DATE/TIME

SPLIT FIBRECAP
Inocybe rimosa

FACT FILE

SIZE Cap diameter 3–7cm; height 3–8cm
HABITAT Associated with deciduous trees such as Beech and oaks
STATUS Widespread and common FRUITING SEASON May–Oct

IDENTIFICATION
Cap is sharply conical, expanding, margin becoming upturned and torn;
surface is radially streaked with brown fibrils on a pale yellow ground.
Gills are olive-yellow. Stem is cylindrical, scurfy, not swollen at base, pale
yellow. Smells spermatic.

COMMENTS
Typically found growing
singly or in small groups
beside paths and on banks
under broadleaved trees such
oaks and Beech, with which
a mycorrhizal partnership
is established.

KEY FACT

The Frosty Fibrecap
Inocybe maculata is similar but has
darker brown fibrils; young specimens
have a frosted appearance thanks to
white remnants of the veil in the
centre of the cap. Both species are
considered to be poisonous.

SPOTTER'S CHART

LOCATION	DATE/TIME

FACT FILE

SIZE **Cap diameter 1–3cm; height 2–5cm**
HABITAT **On the ground mainly in deciduous woodland**
STATUS **Widespread and common** FRUITING SEASON **Aug–Nov**

IDENTIFICATION

Cap is conical to bell-shaped, expanding and flattening with an umbo; silky to finely fibrillose, white with a pale yellow to buff centre. Gills are sinuate; lilaceous, then greyish brown. Stem is cylindrical, sometimes a little swollen at base, silky white.

COMMENTS

Commonly encountered growing in large, scattered groups on the ground under deciduous trees, with which a mycorrhizal partnership is established.

KEY FACT

This species commonly grows together with its beautiful lilac-tinted counterpart, the Lilac Fibrecap *Inocybe geophylla* var. *lilacina*. Both are deadly poisonous.

SPOTTER'S CHART

LOCATION	DATE/TIME

YELLOW FIELDCAP
Bolbitius titubans

FACT FILE

SIZE **Cap diameter 1–5cm; height 3–10cm**
HABITAT **Decaying grass and leaves, old dung and woodchips**
STATUS **Widespread and common** FRUITING SEASON **May–Dec**

KEY FACT

Sometimes a confusing species to identify on account of the potential for the bright yellow colour of the fresh caps to disappear almost completely save for a small area in the centre.

IDENTIFICATION
Cap is egg-shaped, expanding and flattening; margin is striate; surface is smooth, sticky or as if glazed; bright yellow, then almost completely fading or washing out greyish cream with age. Gills are free, crowded; pale yellow, then rusty brown. Stem is cylindrical, white to pale yellow.

COMMENTS
Typically found growing singly or in small groups on dung or in grassland. It tends to be more tufted and robust when growing in compost heaps and on woodchips.

SPOTTER'S CHART

LOCATION	DATE/TIME

FACT FILE

SIZE Cap diameter 2–6cm; height 3–8cm
HABITAT On decayed wood of deciduous and coniferous trees
STATUS Widespread and very common **FRUITING SEASON** Jun–Dec

IDENTIFICATION

Cap is convex, expanding; surface is smooth, cream to sulphur yellow with a more orange centre. Gills are adnate, crowded; greenish yellow, eventually turning purplish black. Stem is cylindrical, curving, fibrillose; sulphur yellow with a transient ring zone near top that becomes stained purplish black with spores.

KEY FACT

A poisonous species that can cause a range of gastro-intestinal upsets. The densely clustered growth habit on decaying wood, together with the greenish-yellow gills that turn purplish black, are useful distinguishing characters.

SPOTTER'S CHART

LOCATION	DATE/TIME

COMMENTS

Very commonly encountered growing in large, dense tufts on stumps and other decaying wood of both deciduous and coniferous trees in summer and autumn.

SHEATHED WOODTUFT
Kuehneromyces mutabilis

FACT FILE

SIZE Cap diameter 2–6cm; height 3–10cm
HABITAT On decaying wood of a wide range of deciduous trees
STATUS Widespread and very common FRUITING SEASON Jun–Nov

IDENTIFICATION
Cap is bluntly bell-shaped with an inrolled margin, eventually expanding and flattening; surface is smooth, hygrophanous, yellowish brown, drying pale yellow in centre. Gills are adnexed; pale buff, becoming rusty. Stem has a ring near apex; brown and scaly below, smooth and pale yellow above. Smells aromatic.

SPOTTER'S CHART

LOCATION	DATE/TIME

KEY FACT
A good edible species, although great care needs to be taken differentiating it from the deadly poisonous Funeral Bell *Galerina marginata*. That species smells mealy and has a fibrillose, not scaly, stem below the ring.

COMMENTS
Almost always found growing in dense, tufted groups on decaying wood of deciduous trees from summer to late autumn.

FACT FILE

SIZE **Cap diameter 5–12cm; height 5–15cm**
HABITAT **At the base of deciduous trees** STATUS **Widespread
and common** FRUITING SEASON **Aug–Dec**

IDENTIFICATION

Cap is hemispherical to bell-shaped, expanding and becoming convex to
broadly bell-shaped; surface is dry, pale yellow, covered in uplifted rusty
scales. Gills are adnate, crowded; pale yellow, later with an olive tint. Stem
is long and curved, pale yellow; covered in uplifted rusty scales below the
high ring zone, smooth above.
Spore deposit is rusty brown.

KEY FACT Confusion is
possible with species of *Armillaria*
such as the Honey Fungus. The
best feature to differentiate
them is spore colour: it is white
in *Armillaria* and rusty brown
in *Pholiota*.

COMMENTS

A splendid large species, almost
always found growing in dense
tufts at the base of living, dying or
recently dead deciduous trees,
especially Beech and Ash.

SPOTTER'S CHART

LOCATION	DATE/TIME

BLUE ROUNDHEAD
Stropharia caerulea

FACT FILE

SIZE **Cap diameter 3–8cm; height 3–10cm**
HABITAT **On nutrient-rich soil in woods, gardens and road verges**
STATUS **Widespread and occasional** FRUITING SEASON **Sep–Nov**

IDENTIFICATION

Cap is convex, slimy; blue-green, fading yellowish from centre out; covered (at least initially) in fleecy white tufts of veil remnants, especially near margin. Gills are adnate; pale, then dark brown. Stem is cylindrical, pale bluish green, with a fleeting ring that may be stained dark brown from spores.

COMMENTS

Typically grows singly or in small groups on nutrient-rich soil in woods and gardens, including on woodchips and mulched flowerbeds; often found with Common Nettles.

KEY FACT

A very variable species that is beautiful and striking when young but dull and dingy when old. It could be confused with the very similar *Stropharia aeruginosa*, but that species has a white edge to the gill.

SPOTTER'S CHART

LOCATION	DATE/TIME

DUNG ROUNDHEAD
Stropharia semiglobata

FACT FILE

SIZE **Cap diameter 1–4cm; height 4–12cm**
HABITAT **On old dung of herbivores and manured soil**
STATUS **Widespread and very common** FRUITING SEASON **May–Dec**

IDENTIFICATION
Cap is hemispherical, slowly expanding and becoming convex but not flat, sometimes with a small umbo; surface is smooth, slimy, straw yellow. Gills are adnate, broad; pale, then dark greyish brown with a greenish tint and white edge. Stem is slender, hollow; slimy and straw yellow below faint ring zone, dry and white above.

KEY FACT The overall straw-yellow colour, slimy cap and distinctive stem help to distinguish Dung Roundhead from a number of other dung-loving species, including *Psilocybe coprophila*, which has a less slimy reddish-brown cap.

COMMENTS
Typically and commonly found growing on old dung of cows and horses and in manured pastures from spring to late autumn, especially after rain.

SPOTTER'S CHART

LOCATION	DATE/TIME

LIBERTY CAP
Psilocybe semilanceata

FACT FILE

SIZE Cap diameter 0.5–2cm; height 4–10cm
HABITAT Mainly acidic grassland, pastures, lawns, parks, playing fields
STATUS Widespread and common **FRUITING SEASON** Aug–Dec

IDENTIFICATION
Cap is distinctly conical with a central pimple, striate; hygrophanous, brown when fresh and moist, soon drying cream. Gills are adnexed; greyish, then dark brown. Stem is slender, wavy; white to brown, sometimes bluish towards base.

KEY FACT Otherwise known as the Magic Mushroom, this well-known and powerful hallucinogenic species has recently been classified as a Class A drug. The active ingredient is psilocybin, which is also present in other members of the group.

COMMENTS
Normally found growing in small groups in short acidic grassland from late summer to winter; especially prevalent after rain.

SPOTTER'S CHART

LOCATION	DATE/TIME

FACT FILE

SIZE **Cap diameter 2–6cm; height 6–15cm**
HABITAT **On dung of herbivores such as cows and horses**
STATUS **Widespread and common** FRUITING SEASON **May–Dec**

IDENTIFICATION

Cap is semi-ovoid to bluntly conical or even bell-shaped; surface is wrinkled and slimy when moist, pale clay coloured. Gills are adnate, crowded, broad; grey, then blackening in patches to give a mottled appearance, edge white. Stem is long, slender and straight, fragile, paler towards apex, and with an ascending ring.

KEY FACT

A distinctive species that should not be confused with any others if the characteristic ovate, wrinkled cap atop a long, straight stem with an upward-pointing ring is observed.

COMMENTS

Commonly encountered growing singly or clustered on cow or horse dung at any time from spring to winter, especially after rain.

SPOTTER'S CHART

LOCATION	DATE/TIME

FIELD MUSHROOM
Agaricus campestris

FACT FILE

SIZE Cap diameter 4–10cm; height 3–6cm
HABITAT Grassland, including pastures, lawns and playing fields
STATUS Widespread and frequent FRUITING SEASON Aug–Nov

IDENTIFICATION
Cap is convex with a strongly inrolled margin when young, often with veil remnants overhanging margin, later expanding and flattening; white to pale greyish brown. Gills are free, crowded; pink, then dark chocolate brown. Stem is short and stout, smooth, white; ring is fragile and easily lost, leaving a faint annular zone.

COMMENTS
A much sought-after edible species that can sometimes be found growing in quite large numbers in meadows and pastures from late summer to early winter.

SPOTTER'S CHART

LOCATION	DATE/TIME

KEY FACT The very similar-looking Cultivated Mushroom *Agaricus bisporus* grows wild in Britain and has the same habitat preference. This has resulted in the two species being much confused, although fortunately both are good edibles.

FACT FILE
SIZE Cap diameter 6–16cm; height 8–12cm
HABITAT Meadows, gardens and grassy areas in open woodland
STATUS Widespread and occasional **FRUITING SEASON** Aug–Dec

IDENTIFICATION

Cap is initially egg-shaped, expanding to convex; smooth; white, then pale brownish yellow when mature, bruising yellow. Gills are pale pink, maturing brown. Stem is cylindrical, base swollen, white; ring is large and floppy with a cogwheel appearance underneath. Flesh is pale yellow when cut and smells of aniseed.

SPOTTER'S CHART

LOCATION	DATE/TIME

KEY FACT

The Yellow Stainer *Agaricus xanthodermus* is a poisonous look-alike that, as its name suggests, quickly bruises bright yellow, especially near the stem base. It has an unpleasant odour, smelling of ink rather than aniseed.

COMMENTS

A much sought-after edible that can be found growing singly or in groups in grassy places such as meadows, parks and road verges from late summer to early winter.

WOOD MUSHROOM
Agaricus silvicola

FACT FILE

SIZE **Cap diameter 5–8cm; height 5–10cm**
HABITAT **On the ground in deciduous and coniferous woods**
STATUS **Widespread and frequent** FRUITING SEASON **Aug–Dec**

IDENTIFICATION
Cap is egg-shaped, expanding and flattening, especially at centre; smooth; cream but soon becoming pale yellow, bruising darker yellow. Gills are free, crowded; pale pink, then chocolate brown. Stem usually has a swollen base; ring is large and floppy. Smells of aniseed.

COMMENTS
Rarely found growing in numbers; more often encountered singly or in small groups in woodland leaf-litter below both hardwoods and conifers.

SPOTTER'S CHART

LOCATION	DATE/TIME

KEY FACT

The Wood Mushroom is, in many respects, the smaller woodland counterpart of the Horse Mushroom and is also edible, but the colour of the gills and presence of an aniseed smell should be confirmed before it is consumed.

FACT FILE

SIZE Cap diameter 2–6cm; height 2–10cm
HABITAT On rich soil in woodlands, parks and gardens
STATUS Widespread and very common **FRUITING SEASON** Jul–Nov

IDENTIFICATION

Cap is hemispherical to convex, covered in radiating woolly fibrils and with remnants of veil hanging from margin; ochre-brown. Gills are mottled dark brown with a white edge and exude small droplets when fresh. Stem is cylindrical with a swollen base and faint ring zone, often stained black from spores.

SPOTTER'S CHART

LOCATION	DATE/TIME

COMMENTS

Normally found in clumps or groups, typically at the edge of paths and roads or in parks, gardens and churchyards from summer to late autumn.

KEY FACT

Features such as the dark weeping gills, the spores staining the ring zone black and the veil remnants hanging from the cap margin help to identify the species and give an understanding of how it received its name.

BROWN MOTTLEGILL
Panaeolina foenisecii

SIZE Cap diameter 2–4cm; height 3–10cm
HABITAT Grassy areas, including meadows, gardens and road verges
STATUS Widespread and very common **FRUITING SEASON** May–Dec

IDENTIFICATION
Cap is hemispherical to convex, finely scurfy; hygrophanous, dark brown when fresh, drying pale straw from centre out and leaving a darker marginal zone. Gills are adnate, fairly crowded, mottled dark chocolate brown. Stem is cylindrical and hollow, pale brown. Spore deposit is dark brown.

KEY FACT
The dark brown spores develop at an uneven rate across the gills, producing a mottled appearance. Interestingly, the gills can also develop swellings, which are actually galls caused by a fruit fly.

COMMENTS
Typically found fruiting in quite large numbers in grassy areas such as meadows and lawns at almost any time of year, but mainly spring to autumn.

SPOTTER'S CHART

LOCATION	DATE/TIME

PALE BRITTLESTEM
Psathyrella candolleana

FACT FILE
SIZE Cap diameter 3–8cm; height 4–10cm
HABITAT On decayed wood and soil in deciduous woodland
STATUS Widespread and common **FRUITING SEASON** May–Dec

KEY FACT
A species that varies considerably during development, especially in cap appearance, with different stages often witnessed within a single group. Numerous related species tend to be darker but still require a microscope to identify correctly.

IDENTIFICATION
Cap is hemispherical, soon expanding and becoming convex; surface has fleeting white veil remnants on an initially reddish-brown ground, then turns ochre; hygrophanous, drying off-white. Gills are crowded; pale buff, maturing dark brown. Stem is white and very fragile; ring is normally absent.

COMMENTS
Often found growing in dense clumps on rotting wood of deciduous trees or on soil in woods or grassy areas from spring to late autumn.

SPOTTER'S CHART

LOCATION	DATE/TIME

COMMON STUMP BRITTLESTEM
Psathyrella piluliformis

FACT FILE

SIZE Cap diameter 2–6cm; height 3–10cm
HABITAT Clustered on decaying wood of deciduous trees
STATUS Widespread and very common FRUITING SEASON Aug–Dec

IDENTIFICATION

Cap is convex; remnants of white veil overhang margin when young and are sometimes seen as fine white streaks on cap surface; hygrophanous, dark reddish brown, fading to tan and drying buff. Gills are adnexed, crowded, white to reddish. Stem is fairly sturdy, hollow, smooth, white.

KEY FACT The almost identical *Psathyrella laevissima* has the same clustered growth habit on decaying wood and a similarly hygrophanous cap, but differs in that it is generally smaller and the veil does not overhang the margin in young specimens.

COMMENTS

Typically found in very dense clusters on decaying wood, especially of Beech and oaks, from summer to early winter.

SPOTTER'S CHART

LOCATION	DATE/TIME

FACT FILE
SIZE Cap diameter 5–15cm; height 5–20cm
HABITAT Lawns, road verges and other open areas
STATUS Widespread and very common FRUITING SEASON Aug–Dec

IDENTIFICATION

Cap is initially elongated egg-shaped and covered in shaggy white tufts, later with edge flaring outwards and deliquescing into a black inky liquid until eventually whole cap dissolves. Gills are white, then pink, finally black and deliquescing. Stem is long, white, with a swollen base and movable ring.

COMMENTS

Frequently found growing alone or in small groups, the species can also be encountered fruiting *en masse*, especially on recently disturbed open areas.

KEY FACT

An interesting feature of this species is that the cap and gills deliquesce, producing a black inky liquid that carries the ripe spores. Gradually the whole cap succumbs, and if picked can dissolve away within a few hours.

SPOTTER'S CHART

LOCATION	DATE/TIME

SNOWY INKCAP
Coprinus niveus

FACT FILE

SIZE Cap diameter 1–3cm; height 3–8cm
HABITAT On dung of herbivores such as cows and horses
STATUS Widespread and common **FRUITING SEASON** Jul–Dec

KEY FACT
Easily recognised when young and fresh by the finely flaky, pure white caps that eventually deliquesce, and the habitat on dung.

IDENTIFICATION
Cap is ovoid, becoming bell-shaped, the edge sometimes splitting as it flares upwards; surface is white and finely flaky from veil. Gills are white, then grey, finally black and deliquescing. Stem is cylindrical, wider at base, white.

COMMENTS
Always found on dung (especially older deposits) of cows, horses, ponies and other herbivores, from summer through autumn.

SPOTTER'S CHART

LOCATION	DATE/TIME

FACT FILE
SIZE **Cap diameter 3–7cm; height 5–15cm**
HABITAT **On decayed and buried wood and roots of deciduous trees**
STATUS **Widespread and common** FRUITING SEASON **Jun–Nov**

IDENTIFICATION

Cap is oval, then conical to bell-shaped and finely grooved, margin becoming split and ragged, finally deliquescing inwards from margin; grey to greyish buff. Gills are free, very crowded; white, then black before deliquescing. Stem is cylindrical and smooth with a fine ring zone low down, white.

KEY FACT

Although edible, this species is best avoided owing to its very unpleasant effects when consumed with alcohol. It contains coprine, which inhibits the breakdown of alcohol in the body, resulting in prolonged hangover symptoms.

COMMENTS

Typically found growing in dense clumps on the ground and arising from buried wood or roots of deciduous trees from spring through autumn.

SPOTTER'S CHART

LOCATION	DATE/TIME

GLISTENING INKCAP
Coprinellus micaceus

SIZE Cap diameter 1–4cm; height 3–10cm
HABITAT On stumps and decaying wood of deciduous trees
STATUS Widespread and very common **FRUITING SEASON** May–Dec

FACT FILE

IDENTIFICATION
Cap is ovoid to bell-shaped; covered in fine, granular veil remnants when young, these wearing off with age and weathering; surface is radially striate, orange-brown in centre, more yellow towards margin. Gills are free, crowded; white, becoming black and deliquescing. Stem is swollen at base, downy, white.

COMMENTS
Very commonly found growing in dense clumps, on or at the base of stumps of deciduous trees, from spring through autumn.

SPOTTER'S CHART

LOCATION	DATE/TIME

KEY FACT

The species' preference for decaying wood, the tightly packed nature of its growth habit and its orange-brown-centred cap, which glistens when young as if sprinkled with mica, are all good clues to aid in its identification.

FACT FILE

SIZE **Cap diameter 1–3cm; height 2–4cm**
HABITAT **On stumps and decayed wood of deciduous trees**
STATUS **Widespread and very common** FRUITING SEASON **May–Dec**

IDENTIFICATION

Cap is ovoid, becoming conical or bell-shaped; surface is covered in fine hairs and granules (hand lens required) and faint grooves; cream, becoming grey with a browner centre; very fragile. Gills are medium-spaced; white, then black but not deliquescing. Stem is hollow and curving, finely downy when young, silvery white.

COMMENTS

The incredibly densely packed and numerous caps, typically clustered on old stumps of deciduous trees, make this otherwise tiny species very conspicuous.

KEY FACT

Psathyrella pygmaea not only looks similar but has the same habitat preference. However, it grows in looser groups and, if viewed with a hand lens, the cap surface is seen to be devoid of both hairs and granules.

SPOTTER'S CHART

LOCATION	DATE/TIME

PLEATED INKCAP
Parasola plicatilis

FACT FILE

SIZE Cap diameter 1–3cm; height 4–12cm
HABITAT In grassland such as lawns and meadows
STATUS Widespread and common FRUITING SEASON May–Dec

KEY FACT

The very delicate nature of the fruit bodies of this species means they can be up and over in less than a day. There are similar species, but the grassland habitat is a good indicator for Pleated Inkcap.

IDENTIFICATION
Cap is ovoid, soon expanding and flattening with grooves or pleats; central disc is orange-brown, elsewhere pale yellow to grey. Gills are not directly attached to stem but to a small collar around it; they do not deliquesce. Stem is tall and slender, off-white to pale yellowish brown.

COMMENTS
Frequently found growing singly or in small groups in short grassy areas such as lawns, especially after rain, from early summer to late autumn.

SPOTTER'S CHART

LOCATION	DATE/TIME

OYSTER MUSHROOM
Pleurotus ostreatus

FACT FILE SIZE Cap diameter 5–15cm HABITAT On living or decaying wood of mainly deciduous trees STATUS Widespread and very common FRUITING SEASON Mainly Sep–Dec

IDENTIFICATION

Cap is shell-shaped with an inrolled margin, expanding and becoming flat to somewhat depressed; surface is smooth, colour varying from dark slate grey to grey-brown or pale greyish yellow. Gills are decurrent, crowded, pale greyish yellow. Stem is attached at one side, rudimentary and sometimes absent, slightly hairy at base, white.

SPOTTER'S CHART

LOCATION	DATE/TIME

KEY FACT

The similar Branching Oyster is deeply funnelled with a longer stem and deeply decurrent gills, while Pale Oyster *Pleurotus pulmonarius* is paler and fruits in summer.

COMMENTS

Usually found fruiting in dense, overlapping tiers on standing or fallen wood of deciduous trees at any time of year, but especially in autumn and well into winter.

BRANCHING OYSTER
Pleurotus cornucopiae

SIZE **Cap diameter 4–15cm** HABITAT **On decaying wood of deciduous trees** STATUS **Widespread and occasional** FRUITING SEASON **Jun–Sep**

KEY FACT The trumpet-shaped caps and network of ridges on the stem are good characters to look for when trying to distinguish this species from some of its similar relatives. The Pale Oyster *Pleurotus pulmonarius* is much flatter and has a rudimentary stem.

IDENTIFICATION
Cap is deeply funnelled or trumpet-shaped, with an inrolled margin that later flattens out; surface is pale yellow-brown, becoming more pallid. Gills are deeply decurrent, shallow, crowded, interconnecting, pale cream. Stem is cylindrical, central or not, with a network of ridges created by interconnecting gills; pale cream.

COMMENTS
Typically occurs densely tufted on standing or fallen trunks and branches of deciduous trees, especially Beech, in summer. The New Forest is a stronghold for the species.

SPOTTER'S CHART

LOCATION	DATE/TIME

COMMON PORECRUST
Schizophyllum commune

FACT FILE   **SIZE** Cap diameter 1–4cm **HABITAT** On dead wood of deciduous trees and hay bales **STATUS** Widespread and common in the S; local elsewhere **FRUITING SEASON** Aug–Mar

IDENTIFICATION

Cap is fan-shaped, with an inrolled margin that often becomes wavy to lobed; very thin-fleshed but tough, densely covered in fine greyish-white hairs. Underside is composed of many split, flesh-coloured, gill-like folds that radiate outward from point of attachment with woody substrate. Stem is either rudimentary or absent.

COMMENTS

Typically encountered fruiting in dense, overlapping tiers on dead wood of deciduous trees or on bales of hay and straw, especially through tears in those wrapped in plastic.

KEY FACT

Schizophyllum literally translates as 'split-leaf' and refers to the gill-like folds on the underside of the fungus, which are split along their length and give this species a unique character by which to identify it.

SPOTTER'S CHART

LOCATION	DATE/TIME

PEELING OYSTERLING
Crepidotus mollis

FACT FILE

SIZE **Cap diameter 1–6cm** HABITAT **On standing or fallen dead wood of deciduous trees** STATUS **Widespread and common** FRUITING SEASON **Aug–Dec**

IDENTIFICATION

Cap is kidney-shaped with an elastic, peelable gelatinous layer that is sometimes smooth and sometimes scaly; ochre-brown to almost white when dry or drying. Gills are crowded and radiate out from point of attachment; pale cream, then greyish brown. Stem is absent or rudimentary, attached to substrate at one edge of cap.

COMMENTS

Fruits singly or in groups on dead standing and fallen wood of deciduous trees, mainly in the autumn but can be found at any time of year.

SPOTTER'S CHART

LOCATION	DATE/TIME

KEY FACT

The Peeling Oysterling is best identified by the gelatinous layer covering the cap surface, which is both elastic and peelable. This character, combined with the species' larger size, help separate it from most of its smaller relatives.

FACT FILE

SIZE Cap diameter 1–4cm; height 2–5cm

HABITAT On woody debris such as twigs and woodchips

STATUS Widespread and common **FRUITING SEASON** Mainly Sep–Jan

KEY FACT

This otherwise plain species attracts attention when it fruits en masse on woodchips. This provides an opportunity to observe its different states, with some specimens showing veil remnants around the cap margin and others creamy dried caps.

IDENTIFICATION

Cap is convex, soon flattening; translucently striate, sometimes with white veil remnants forming a narrow broken band around margin; orange-brown, drying cream. Gills are adnate, sometimes with a decurrent tooth, medium-spaced, buff. Stem is hollow, buff, with white down often evident at base.

SPOTTER'S CHART

LOCATION	DATE/TIME

COMMENTS

Fruits singly, in groups or, in extreme cases, in great swarms over woodchips and mulch beds, especially in winter.

CHANTERELLE
Cantharellus cibarius

FACT FILE

SIZE Cap diameter 3–10cm; height 3–8cm
HABITAT Associated with deciduous trees STATUS Widespread
and common FRUITING SEASON Aug–Nov

IDENTIFICATION
Cap is convex, soon expanding and developing a depressed centre,
finally funnel-shaped; surface is rather undulating with a wavy to
lobed margin; rich golden yellow.
Gills are ridge-like with numerous
forks and interconnections, deeply
decurrent, concolourous with cap
or paler. Stem is short, merging
into cap. Smells faintly of apricots.

COMMENTS
Fruits singly or in small to large
groups under old deciduous trees
such as birches, Beech and
oaks, with which it forms a
mycorrhizal partnership.

> **KEY FACT**
> A highly
> prized and sought-after edible
> that is said to be declining across
> Europe. Confusion is possible
> with the very common False
> Chanterelle, but that species has
> bright orange gills and grows in
> needle-litter under pines.

SPOTTER'S CHART

LOCATION	DATE/TIME

FACT FILE

SIZE Fruit-body diameter 2–7cm; height 3–12cm
HABITAT In moss or soil in deciduous woodland
STATUS Widespread and occasional FRUITING SEASON Sep–Nov

IDENTIFICATION

Fruit body is an elongated, thin-walled, hollow trumpet with a downturned, wavy edge. Inner surface is roughened by fine scales or fibrils, dark brown to black. Outer surface is smooth to wrinkled, pale grey, blacker towards base. Smells faintly aromatic, sweet and pleasant.

KEY FACT

A good edible that can be surprisingly difficult to spot on the woodland floor, but when found is hardly likely to be confused with anything else.

COMMENTS

Normally encountered fruiting gregariously, with many fruit bodies tightly packed together in moss or leaf-litter under deciduous trees in autumn.

SPOTTER'S CHART

LOCATION	DATE/TIME

FALSE CHANTERELLE
Hygrophoropsis aurantiaca

FACT FILE

SIZE **Cap diameter 3–6cm; height 3–8cm**
HABITAT **In needle-litter or on woody debris of conifers**
STATUS **Widespread and very common** FRUITING SEASON **Aug–Jan**

IDENTIFICATION
Cap is convex, later becoming depressed in centre and wavy-edged, margin inrolled for some time; surface is softly suede-like, colour varying from bright orange to pale yellowish, sometimes with a greenish tinge. Gills are deeply decurrent, narrow and forking, bright orange. Stem is cylindrical, often curving; concolourous with cap or a shade darker.

SPOTTER'S CHART

LOCATION	DATE/TIME

KEY FACT

Cap colour is very variable, which can lead to much confusion, but the gills usually remain bright orange, a feature that helps to separate it from the Chanterelle. Best avoided as some consider it to be poisonous.

COMMENTS
Typically found growing in troops in needle-litter or decaying woody debris under conifers, usually from late summer to winter.

DRYAD'S SADDLE
Polyporus squamosus

FACT FILE

SIZE Bracket width 10–50cm; height 10–30cm
HABITAT On decaying wood and wound sites of deciduous trees
STATUS Widespread and common **FRUITING SEASON** Jun–Sep

IDENTIFICATION

Brackets are circular to fan-shaped, growing in overlapping tiers; surface is covered in large brown scales arranged concentrically on a pale creamy ground. Tubes are decurrent. Pores are large and angular, irregularly shaped, creamy white. Stem is attached from one side or off-centre, short and thick, blackening at base.

SPOTTER'S CHART

LOCATION	DATE/TIME

KEY FACT

The large angular, irregular pores running down the stem, together with the conspicuously scaly cap and blackening of the stem base in mature specimens, are useful identification characters.

COMMENTS

A parasitic species of deciduous trees that fruits from ground level to high up on standing trunks in the summer.

HAIRY CURTAIN CRUST
Stereum hirsutum

FACT FILE

SIZE Bracket width 1–3cm HABITAT On attached or
fallen branches and trunks of deciduous trees STATUS Widespread
and very common FRUITING SEASON Jul–Dec

IDENTIFICATION
Individual brackets
are thin and leathery,
irregularly semicircular,
attached to wood as if
glued on; upper surface is
undulating, densely hairy,
zoned in various shades of
brown, orange, yellow or
even green towards centre
from algae formation in
older specimens. Lower
surface is smooth,
yellowish orange.

COMMENTS
Typically encountered fruiting
en masse in overlapping tiers,
with individual brackets fusing
with nearby neighbours, on fallen
branches of deciduous trees in
the summer.

KEY FACT A useful
character in separating this from
several other similar and related
species is the non-bleeding pore
surface when cut or scored.

SPOTTER'S CHART

LOCATION	DATE/TIME

BLEEDING OAK CRUST
Stereum gausapatum

FACT FILE
SIZE Bracket width 1–4cm HABITAT On fallen and attached branches of oaks STATUS Widespread and common FRUITING SEASON Aug–Dec

IDENTIFICATION
At times wholly resupinate, forming irregular patches, or can develop thin, leathery, wavy-edged brackets that fuse together in overlapping tiers. Upper surface is hairy, zoned in various shades of reddish brown with a whitish margin. Lower surface is orange-brown with a whitish margin, bleeding red when cut or scored.

COMMENTS
Almost always encountered fruiting en masse in overlapping and fused patches or brackets on fallen branches of oaks from summer through autumn.

KEY FACT
The species' preference for oak limbs, combined with its propensity to bleed red when cut or scored, help to separate it from similar brackets such as the Hairy Curtain Crust.

SPOTTER'S CHART

LOCATION	DATE/TIME

WHITE SPINDLES
Clavaria fragilis

FACT FILE

SIZE **Height 2–10cm** HABITAT **Unimproved grassland** STATUS **Widespread and common** FRUITING SEASON **Sep–Dec**

IDENTIFICATION
Normally consists of a densely tufted clump of unbranched, spindle-like white fruit bodies. Individual fruit bodies are upright, straight or wavy, cylindrical or flattened, hollow and sometimes grooved lengthways, and usually have a pointed tip that yellows with age. Flesh is very brittle.

COMMENTS
Typically encountered growing in dense tufts of white spindles in fairly short turf in unimproved grassland.

KEY FACT

An easy species to recognise, but there are potential identification pitfalls. Pointed Club *Clavaria acuta* is also white but tends to grow singly, and a number of yellow species could cause confusion when washed out.

SPOTTER'S CHART

LOCATION	DATE/TIME

FACT FILE

SIZE Height 3–15cm HABITAT Grassland on acid ground such as heaths, moors and gardens STATUS Widespread and common FRUITING SEASON Sep–Nov

IDENTIFICATION

Consists of a densely tufted clump of unbranched, bright golden-yellow spindle- to club-shaped fruit bodies fused at base. Individual fruit bodies are upright, straight or a little wavy, sometimes slightly twisted, cylindrical or flattened, often grooved lengthways, with a pointed or blunt tip that browns with age.

KEY FACT Typically, this is a much larger and more densely tufted species than other yellow spindle-like species that may be encountered in the same habitat. Meadow Coral is also densely tufted but is rather wavy and much branched.

COMMENTS

The golden-yellow clumps can be found throughout the autumn in grassy areas that have not recently been ploughed or fertilised.

SPOTTER'S CHART

LOCATION	DATE/TIME

MEADOW CORAL
Clavulinopsis corniculata

FACT FILE

SIZE **Height 2–6cm** HABITAT **Grassland, including lawns, parks and cricket pitches** STATUS **Widespread and very common** FRUITING SEASON **Sep–Jan**

IDENTIFICATION
Fruit body is coral-like, tufted, repeatedly branching from a common base. Branches are wavy, topped with multiple incurving tips, wholly yellow to ochre-yellow with white mycelial down at very base. Flesh is tough, pale yellow; tastes bitter and smells slightly mealy.

COMMENTS
A very common grassland species that is not restricted to, but has a preference for, unimproved turf and is typically found fruiting in scattered groups in the autumn.

KEY FACT

Similar-looking yellow coral-like species include the Yellow Stagshorn, but that is bright yellow with gelatinous flesh and grows on stumps and other decaying wood of conifers.

SPOTTER'S CHART

LOCATION	DATE/TIME

FACT FILE SIZE **Height 4–8cm** HABITAT **On buried wood of deciduous trees, woodchips, mulch beds** STATUS **Widespread and frequent** FRUITING SEASON **Aug–Dec**

IDENTIFICATION

Fruit body is coral-like with many ascending branches, giving it a very upright appearance. Individual branches are usually fused at base and branch repeatedly as they ascend; buff to flesh coloured with yellowish tips when young, bruising dark purplish brown. Flesh is tough. Smells sweet.

COMMENTS

Traditionally found on buried or partly buried sticks and branches of deciduous trees in woodland. Nowadays, it is just as frequently encountered on woodchips.

KEY FACT

There are several species with which Upright Coral may be confused. Good indicators are its very upright appearance as it arises from wood; the fleshy colour, bruising darker purplish brown; and the strong, sweet smell.

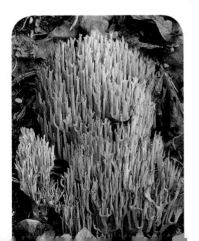

SPOTTER'S CHART

LOCATION	DATE/TIME

WOOD CAULIFLOWER
Sparassis crispa

FACT FILE

SIZE Diameter 10–40cm; height 10–25cm
HABITAT At the base of conifer trees such as Scots Pine
STATUS Widespread and common FRUITING SEASON Sep–Nov

IDENTIFICATION
Fruit body is cauliflower- or brain-like, made up of many tightly packed wavy and crispy leaf-like lobes arising from numerous radiating branches that are ultimately connected to a thick, rooting inner stem that is visible only if fungus is broken apart. Overall colour is cream to buff, becoming browner with age.

KEY FACT
A very distinctive species, unlikely to be mistaken for anything else apart from its close relative *Sparassis spathulata*, which is rare and prefers fruiting at the base of deciduous trees, although is not restricted to them.

COMMENTS
Nearly always found fruiting at the base of living or recently dead conifer trees. It is initially parasitic on the roots and then saprotrophic once the tree is dead.

SPOTTER'S CHART

LOCATION	DATE/TIME

SIZE **Height 5–18cm** HABITAT **In deciduous and coniferous woodland, gardens, sand-dunes** STATUS **Widespread and very common** FRUITING SEASON **Mainly Aug–Dec**

KEY FACT

Visiting flies are attracted by the putrid, carrion-like smell of the slimy cap coating. The spore-laden slime adheres to their legs as they walk on the cap surface, and is then dispersed when they fly off and land elsewhere.

IDENTIFICATION

Immature fruit body is a whitish 'egg' attached to a cord of white mycelium. Mature fruit body is phallus-like. Cap is bell-shaped, initially covered in a greenish-brown putrid-smelling slime that is soon dispersed by visiting flies to reveal a creamy network of ridges beneath. Stem is tubular.

COMMENTS

When conditions are right, the developing fruit body pierces the skin of the partly submerged 'egg' and thrusts skywards, forming the mature Stinkhorn within a matter of hours.

SPOTTER'S CHART

LOCATION	DATE/TIME

DOG STINKHORN
Mutinus caninus

FACT FILE

SIZE Height 4–12cm HABITAT Soil or rotting wood in deciduous woodland, woodchips STATUS Widespread and common; scarcer further N FRUITING SEASON Aug–Dec

IDENTIFICATION
Immature fruit body is an off-white 'egg' a few centimetres across and partly submerged. Mature fruit body is spike-like, its orange tip soon revealed after the putrid, dark olive covering slime is dispersed by flies. Stem is tubular, gently curving upwards from within egg, densely pitted, pale cream to orange.

COMMENTS
Traditionally encountered close to or on rotting wood of deciduous trees in woodland, the species has recently become frequent on woodchips and mulched flowerbeds.

KEY FACT Similar to, but much smaller than, the Stinkhorn; it also differs significantly in that the stem merges almost seamlessly into the tip (the Stinkhorn has a distinctly separate cap).

SPOTTER'S CHART

LOCATION	DATE/TIME

YELLOW STAGSHORN
Calocera viscosa

FACT FILE

SIZE Height 2–6cm HABITAT Dead wood of conifers, especially stumps STATUS Widespread and very common FRUITING SEASON Sep–Jan

IDENTIFICATION

Fruit body is coral-like, comprising multiple antler-like branches, these typically forking at very tips and arising from a common base that is securely attached to substrate; surface is greasy to slimy; yellow when fresh, drying orange. Flesh is tough and gelatinous.

KEY FACT Although coral-like, the Yellow Stagshorn is not related to the coral fungi. Distinguishing features are the greasy to viscid surface and tough gelatinous flesh, which contrasts with the brittle, dry, non-gelatinous flesh of the corals.

COMMENTS

A very common fungus in autumn and early winter in conifer woodland; it has a preference for stumps and fallen, rotten trunks, into which it roots strongly.

SPOTTER'S CHART

LOCATION	DATE/TIME

WITCHES' BUTTER
Exidia glandulosa

FACT FILE

SIZE Diameter 2–5cm HABITAT On attached or
fallen twigs, branches and trunks of deciduous trees
STATUS Widespread and very common FRUITING SEASON Aug–Jan

IDENTIFICATION
Disc- to button-shaped cushions, becoming irregularly lobed and often
fusing with neighbours. Whole fruit body is black, fertile lower surface
covered in tiny pimples, upper surface velvety. Flesh is gelatinous, firm and
jelly-like to touch, shrivelling in
dry weather and reconstituting
when wet.

KEY FACT
Frequently
confused with its close relative
Exidia plana, but that species is
much more folded and wrinkled,
and often forms extensive
brain-like patches. Leafy Brain
fungus *Tremella foliacea* is brown
and even more lobed and jelly-like.

COMMENTS
Typically encountered in late
autumn and winter on fallen
twigs and branches of deciduous
trees such as oak and Hazel,
especially after strong winds.

SPOTTER'S CHART

LOCATION	DATE/TIME

FACT FILE

SIZE **Diameter 10–50cm** HABITAT **At the base of deciduous trees, especially oaks** STATUS **Widespread and occasional in S England, rare elsewhere** FRUITING SEASON **Aug–Nov**

KEY FACT
The Giant Polypore *Meripilus giganteus* is superficially similar and produces even larger composite fruit bodies, but the individual brackets are fan-shaped rather than tongue-shaped and all parts blacken when bruised.

IDENTIFICATION

A large compound structure consisting of numerous densely overlapping, tongue-shaped, leathery brackets arising from a central stem. Upper surface is streaked with grey to brown radiating fibres on a pale background. Lower surface is covered in small, decurrent off-white pores that mature light brown. Smell is pleasant at first, then increasingly reminiscent of mice urine.

COMMENTS

This species is parasitic on the roots of old deciduous trees. It typically fruits at the base of old oaks but can occur with other hardwoods, including Sweet Chestnut.

SPOTTER'S CHART

LOCATION	DATE/TIME

DYER'S MAZEGILL
Phaeolus schweinitzii

FACT FILE

SIZE Diameter 10–50cm; height 5–20cm
HABITAT Mainly at the base of old conifers, especially Scots Pine
STATUS Widespread and common FRUITING SEASON Aug–Dec

IDENTIFICATION
Initially a shapeless, spongy yellow lump, gradually expanding to form irregular, horizontal, fan- to plate-shaped brackets, sometimes overlapping and connected to a central stem. Upper surface is hairy, reddish brown with a yellow margin. Lower surface bears irregular, maze-like greenish-yellow pores that bruise dark brown.

KEY FACT
An annual fungus that produces new fruit bodies each year, these gradually decaying and disintegrating before the following year's fruiting. A yellow-brown pigment was once extracted from fresh specimens to dye wool and cloth.

COMMENTS
Parasitic on the roots of many species of conifer, Dyer's Mazegill is usually found growing close to the base of the trunk, making it appear terrestrial.

SPOTTER'S CHART

LOCATION	DATE/TIME

CHICKEN OF THE WOODS
Laetiporus sulphureus

FACT FILE

SIZE Bracket width 10–40cm, depth 1–2cm
HABITAT Mainly on old deciduous trees, especially oaks
STATUS Widespread and very common FRUITING SEASON Jun–Sep

IDENTIFICATION
Initially simple bright yellow to orange swellings that gradually morph into the more familiar fan-shaped brackets. Mature fruit bodies are arranged in a series of dense, overlapping tiers, bright sulphur yellow to bright orange when fresh. Older specimens fade to off-white and become crumbly.

COMMENTS
Initially parasitic, the fungus fruits on living trees in summer, with the brackets sometimes quite high up on the trunk.

KEY FACT A familiar species on account of its bright colours, and unlikely to be confused with anything else except perhaps the Giant Polypore *Meripilus giganteus*. However, that species always fruits at the base of trunks and has more sombre colours.

SPOTTER'S CHART

LOCATION	DATE/TIME

ROOT ROT
Heterobasidion annosum

FACT FILE

SIZE Bracket length 5–25cm, width 5–10cm, depth 1–3cm **HABITAT** At the base of stumps and trunks of conifer trees **STATUS** Widespread and very common **FRUITING SEASON** Jul–Nov

IDENTIFICATION
Very variable, sometimes forming brackets and sometimes resupinate. Upper surface of brackets is uneven to bumpy; rusty brown, contrasting strongly with white margin that often surrounds an adjacent brighter reddish-orange band. Lower surface is white and covered in tiny pores (two to four per millimetre). Smells strong and fungus-like.

KEY FACT The species is a serious problem in conifer plantations, where it causes a brown rot. Spores landing on freshly cut stumps develop, and once established can spread to adjacent trees via their root systems.

COMMENTS
Parasitic on the roots of conifers, and usually found fruiting at the very base of stumps or trunks of infected trees.

SPOTTER'S CHART

LOCATION	DATE/TIME

BIRCH POLYPORE
Piptoporus betulinus

FACT FILE

SIZE Bracket width 5–20cm, depth 2–7cm
HABITAT On standing and fallen birch trunks and logs
STATUS Widespread and very common **FRUITING SEASON** Jan–Dec

IDENTIFICATION
Initially a simple whitish knob, expanding to form a rubbery, kidney-shaped bracket with a thick, rounded margin that is white while growing. Sterile upper surface is smooth; various shades of brown, showing white where scratched. Fertile lower surface is white and covered in minute pores. Smells fragrant.

COMMENTS
Parasitic on, and totally restricted, to birch trees. It is almost always present wherever birches occur and can be found at any time of year.

SPOTTER'S CHART

LOCATION	DATE/TIME

KEY FACT
Although not edible, the species has nevertheless been put to many good uses over the years. Its alternative common name of Razor Strop indicates that it was once used to help sharpen razors by polishing their edges.

HOOF FUNGUS
Fomes fomentarius

FACT FILE

SIZE Bracket width 5–40cm, depth 5–25cm
HABITAT Standing trunks of decaying deciduous trees
STATUS Widespread and common FRUITING SEASON Jan–Dec

IDENTIFICATION
Perennial woody bracket, becoming more hoof-shaped as new tube layers are added each year. Upper surface has a hard crust, concentrically grooved and zoned in shades of grey, and with a white margin in times of growth. Fertile lower surface is pale grey, discolouring brownish with age and darkening when handled.

COMMENTS
In Scotland and N England the species is common on standing birches, but in the S it is much less frequent and usually found on Beech or Sycamore.

KEY FACT

The perennial nature and ability of the Hoof Fungus to add a new tube layer each year gives rise to its common name. It is also known as the Tinder Fungus, as it burns slowly and is useful for starting fires.

SPOTTER'S CHART

LOCATION	DATE/TIME

BLUSHING BRACKET
Daedaleopsis confragosa

FACT FILE　　**SIZE** Bracket length 6–15cm, width 4–8cm, depth
1–3cm **HABITAT** On decaying wood of deciduous trees
STATUS Widespread and very common **FRUITING SEASON** Jun–Dec

IDENTIFICATION

Individual brackets are semicircular. Upper surface is flat, smooth or lumpy; often concentrically banded, though colours vary from creamy white to buff and often dark reddish brown, especially when wet. Lower surface bears round to slot-like pores; white, then more dingy grey-brown, bruising reddish.

KEY FACT The reddish discoloration of the pore surface of fresher specimens when rubbed gives rise to the species' common name and is a useful characteristic in identifying it, especially as the upper surface is so variable.

COMMENTS

Occurs singly or, more usually, in groups, with brackets persisting throughout the year on dead branches and trunks of deciduous trees such as birches and willows.

SPOTTER'S CHART

LOCATION	DATE/TIME

OAK MAZEGILL
Daedalea quercina

SIZE Bracket length 8–20cm, width 6–12 cm, depth 2–5cm **HABITAT** On decaying oaks and Sweet Chestnut **STATUS** Widespread and common **FRUITING SEASON** Jun–Dec

FACT FILE

IDENTIFICATION
Individual bracket is semicircular, corky, often fusing with others nearby. Upper surface is uneven, sometimes concentrically zoned in pale shades of buff and ochre. Lower surface bears deep maze-like pores with thick walls, these sometimes appearing almost gill-like; pale creamy buff.

SPOTTER'S CHART

LOCATION	DATE/TIME

COMMENTS
Persisting for several years, the brackets usually occur tiered and fused on stumps and standing or fallen trunks of oak and Sweet Chestnut.

KEY FACT
The maze-like underside is quite distinct and hence a good indicator of this species. Confusion with the Blushing Bracket is possible, but that species is less robust and has round to slot-like pores that bruise reddish.

FACT FILE

SIZE Bracket length 1–4cm, width 1–2cm, depth 1–2mm **HABITAT** On dead conifer wood **STATUS** Widespread and very common **FRUITING SEASON** Sep–Jan

IDENTIFICATION

Individual brackets are semicircular and very thin. Upper surface is felty, concentrically grooved; pale greyish, later staining green with algae, and often with one or two thin concentric bands of purple nearer margin. Lower surface is covered in small angular pores that become ragged with age; initially bright purple, soon turning brown and fading.

COMMENTS

Typically found fruiting afresh in late autumn to winter in rows or tiers of fused brackets in crevices on branches, trunks and stumps of various conifers.

KEY FACT Persisting throughout the year, this species is relatively easy to identify when fresh thanks to the vivid purple colour of the underside and cap margin, but it is worth remembering that this indicator can be completely missing at other times.

SPOTTER'S CHART

LOCATION	DATE/TIME

TURKEYTAIL
Trametes versicolor

FACT FILE

SIZE Bracket length 3–10cm, width 3–8cm, depth 1–3mm HABITAT On stumps, logs and other wood of deciduous trees STATUS Widespread and very common FRUITING SEASON Jan–Dec

IDENTIFICATION
Individual brackets are semicircular, thin yet tough. Upper surface is felty; markedly concentrically zoned with alternating light and dark narrow bands of a wide range of colours, though typically with a white growing margin and green algal staining when older. Lower surface is white, with two to four pores per millimetre.

COMMENTS
A beautiful year-round species, found clustered in overlapping and fused groups on stumps and logs of many deciduous trees.

KEY FACT
Although inedible, this species has proven immune system-enhancing and anti-cancer properties. An extract marketed as 'Coriolus' is now being widely used as a part of cancer therapy in many western countries.

SPOTTER'S CHART

LOCATION	DATE/TIME

SMOKY BRACKET
Bjerkandera adusta

FACT FILE SIZE Bracket length 2–5cm, width 1–4cm, depth 3–5mm HABITAT On dead and dying deciduous trees STATUS Widespread and common FRUITING SEASON Jan–Dec

IDENTIFICATION

Initially forms small resupinate patches with a grey centre and white border, later develops rubbery brackets. Upper surface is wavy, felty, concentrically zoned, grey-brown. Lower surface is covered in minute spore-bearing pores, smoky grey with a white margin while growing.

COMMENTS

This species causes a white rot and typically fruits in dense clusters of tiered and fused brackets on dead or dying wood, especially stumps of Beech and birches.

KEY FACT

The Big Smoky Bracket *Bjerkandera fumosa* is similar, but is scarcer and larger, and has a paler pore surface and a preference for Sycamore stumps.

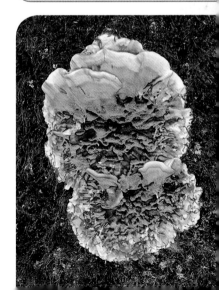

SPOTTER'S CHART

LOCATION	DATE/TIME

ARTIST'S BRACKET
Ganoderma applanatum

FACT FILE

SIZE Bracket length 10–50cm, width 10–30cm, depth 1–4cm HABITAT On trunks of deciduous trees, especially Beech STATUS Widespread and occasional FRUITING SEASON Jan–Dec

IDENTIFICATION
Bracket is robust, semicircular. Upper surface is often lumpy or wrinkled, concentrically grooved, with a hard lacquered crust; pale-grey-buff but usually stained rusty brown from spores. Lower surface is covered in minute pores; white, bruising brown.

KEY FACT

The white pore-bearing lower surface easily marks brown when touched, giving rise to the species' common name. Nipple-shaped galls can sometimes be found protruding downwards and are formed by the larvae of the fly *Agathomyia wankowiczii*.

COMMENTS
The large shelf-like brackets persist for many years and cause a white rot in several species of deciduous trees and, more rarely, in conifers.

SPOTTER'S CHART

LOCATION	DATE/TIME

COMMON PUFFBALL
Lycoperdon perlatum

FACT FILE

SIZE **Head diameter 2–6cm; height 3–8cm**
HABITAT **On the ground, mainly in deciduous woods**
STATUS **Widespread and very common** FRUITING SEASON **Aug–Nov**

IDENTIFICATION
Fruit body is pear-shaped, with a bulb-like head on a distinct stem; white. Fertile head containing developing spores is densely covered in small white pyramidal warts that wear off in time, leaving an indistinct network pattern. At maturity, a central pore develops to allow release of mature spores within.

KEY FACT The spores develop inside the head on a structure called the gleba. At maturity, raindrops cause the wall of the bulb to compress slightly, increasing the pressure within and forcing the spores up through the central pore.

COMMENTS
Although commonly encountered on the ground in deciduous woods in autumn, the species has recently started to colonise woodchips, where it may fruit in abundance.

SPOTTER'S CHART

LOCATION	DATE/TIME

STUMP PUFFBALL
Lycoperdon pyriforme

FACT FILE

SIZE Head diameter 2–4 cm; height 3–6cm
HABITAT On decaying wood of deciduous trees, especially stumps
STATUS Widespread and very common FRUITING SEASON Aug–Dec

IDENTIFICATION

Fruit body is pear- or club-shaped; white at first, becoming buff or brown. Head is covered in fine spines or warts that easily rub off, and develops a darker brown central area. At maturity, a pore opens centrally to release spores. Stem is short and spongy, tapering at base, where it is attached to substrate via long mycelial strands.

COMMENTS

Grows in distinctive dense clusters, especially on the stumps of deciduous trees, and is very common in autumn.

SPOTTER'S CHART

LOCATION	DATE/TIME

KEY FACT
The spent fruit bodies often persist for some time – it is not uncommon to find them the following spring, though they are usually in a rather poor state by then.

FACT FILE SIZE Diameter 10–70cm HABITAT Nutrient-rich sites in fields, parks and gardens STATUS Widespread and occasional FRUITING SEASON Jun–Oct

IDENTIFICATION

Ball-like, though usually misshapen, size varying from a cricket ball to a football or even a beach ball. Surface is initially smooth and white, flesh firm and white. All parts discolour brownish, surface disintegrating to expose mature soft, spongy brown spore-laden mass within. Connected directly to substrate via cord-like mycelial strands.

COMMENTS

Fruiting often begins in early summer, usually gregariously in groups or rings in nitrogen-rich sites such as Common Nettle beds and compost heaps.

KEY FACT Only young fruit bodies are edible, when the flesh is white and firm throughout. The mature spongy brown fruit bodies may often become detached and be blown around, helping to scatter the millions of spores.

SPOTTER'S CHART

LOCATION	DATE/TIME

MEADOW PUFFBALL
Vascellum pratense

FACT FILE

SIZE Diameter 2–4cm; height 2–5cm HABITAT Short turf in open areas, including lawns STATUS Widespread and very common FRUITING SEASON Jun–Nov

IDENTIFICATION
Spinning top-shaped, with a rounded, flat-topped head and short, tapering base. Head is initially white to cream and covered in fine spines, later yellowing, and finally brown with a large circular opening at apex to release spores. Base is sterile and separated from fertile head by a thin membrane.

COMMENTS
Typically found fruiting in summer, either singly or, more commonly, in small groups in very short turf in open areas practically anywhere.

KEY FACT

The characteristic feature of this species is the thin membrane separating the fertile head from the sterile base, but this is only really visible in longitudinal cross section.

SPOTTER'S CHART

LOCATION	DATE/TIME

FACT FILE

SIZE Diameter 4–12cm HABITAT Associated with deciduous trees on acidic soils STATUS Widespread and very common FRUITING SEASON Jul–Nov

IDENTIFICATION

Rounded to potato-shaped, hard and covered in many brown scales on a dingy yellowish background. Outer skin is up to 5mm thick and completely encloses black spore-developing mass inside. Over time, skin rots and cracks, exposing mature spores within. Smells strongly and distinctively of rubber.

COMMENTS

A very common and familiar species appearing in summer on heathland and other acidic ground. It is associated with hardwood trees such as birches and Beech.

SPOTTER'S CHART

LOCATION	DATE/TIME

KEY FACT

Surprisingly, it has recently been found that earthballs are in fact closely related to boletes. This discovery was made using DNA sequencing, which is unearthing many strange alliances between species that were previously thought to be unrelated.

COLLARED EARTHSTAR
Geastrum triplex

FACT FILE

SIZE Overall diameter 5–12cm; spore sac 2–4cm
HABITAT In leaf-litter and compost heaps STATUS Widespread
and common FRUITING SEASON Sep–Dec

IDENTIFICATION
Initially bulb-like, outer skin then splitting into four to eight rays that arch back in unison, revealing and lifting inner spore-bearing sac upwards and clear of ground while often forming a distinct collar encircling it. Spore sac is smooth and thin-walled, with a small fibrous apical pore with a pale halo.

KEY FACT
Spores are dispersed through the apical pore by the pressure exerted from raindrops hitting and compressing the thin wall of the containing sac. Wind currents over the pore also cause spores to be released.

COMMENTS
Usually found fruiting in groups or rings in nutrient-rich places such as leaf-litter, compost heaps and mulched flowerbeds.

SPOTTER'S CHART

LOCATION	DATE/TIME

FACT FILE
SIZE Cup diameter 5–12mm **HABITAT** Woody debris and herbaceous plant stems **STATUS** Widespread and common in the S; occasional elsewhere **FRUITING SEASON** Sep–Dec

IDENTIFICATION

At first cushion-shaped, with a densely hairy yellow lid-like membrane that is eventually lost to reveal a cup-shaped structure with a smooth, shiny inner surface holding around 8–12 lentil-shaped white eggs, each about 2mm across and attached to base of 'nest' via a thread-like cord.

KEY FACT

The Fluted Bird's Nest *Cyathus striatus* is steeply conical, with a grooved inner surface and densely brown hairy outer surface. The Field Bird's Nest *C. olla* is also a conical fungus, but is much shallower and lacks striations.

COMMENTS

Conspicuous only when fruiting en masse, the species is best looked for on woodchips and mulched areas in flowerbeds in parks and gardens.

SPOTTER'S CHART

LOCATION	DATE/TIME

CORAL TOOTH
Hericium coralloides

FACT FILE

SIZE Diameter 6–30cm HABITAT Almost exclusively on standing, rotting trunks of Beech STATUS Very local and rare FRUITING SEASON Sep–Nov

IDENTIFICATION
Fruit body is coral-like and much branched from a more or less central trunk. Each branch is covered in numerous 1cm-long, mainly downward-pointing spines or 'teeth', these carrying the spore-bearing structures. Whole structure is pure white at first, discolouring yellowish to brownish later.

COMMENTS
A rare and beautiful species, best looked for on well-decayed but still standing trunks of Beech. Even in its New Forest stronghold it is hard to find and should not be collected.

KEY FACT

This species is one of the tooth fungi, so called on account of their tooth-like spinal projections. The Bearded Tooth *Hericium erinaceum* also grows on Beech but has much longer and more densely packed spines.

SPOTTER'S CHART

LOCATION	DATE/TIME

FACT FILE

SIZE **Cap diameter 0.5–2cm; height 2–6cm**
HABITAT **Almost exclusively on pinecones**
STATUS **Widespread and common** FRUITING SEASON **Jan–Dec**

IDENTIFICATION

Cap is kidney-shaped, finely but densely hairy, reddish brown to dark brown with a paler margin. Underside is covered in downward-pointing spines a few millimetres in length and pale grey. Stem is attached to one side of cap, tough and densely hairy, reddish brown to dark brown, arising directly from cone.

COMMENTS

Easily overlooked and best looked for in damper areas under pines or after a good period of rain, as this helps stimulate fruiting.

KEY FACT

This unique and distinctive species is easily overlooked on account of its size and colour, and because its pinecone host may be partially or fully buried in needle-litter.

SPOTTER'S CHART

LOCATION	DATE/TIME

BEEFSTEAK FUNGUS
Fistulina hepatica

FACT FILE

SIZE Bracket width 5–25cm, depth 2–5cm
HABITAT On trunks of oaks and Sweet Chestnut
STATUS Widespread and common FRUITING SEASON Aug–Oct

KEY FACT
An important character distinguishing this species from other polypores is that its tubes can easily be separated from one another when young; when older, they begin to stick together somewhat.

IDENTIFICATION
Initially a soft, bright pinkish knob, developing into a tongue- or kidney-shaped bracket. Upper surface is moist, blood red and oozing reddish drops. Lower surface is covered in pores; initially pale yellow, reddening with age. Flesh is succulent; red with lighter veining, giving it a marbled appearance when cut.

SPOTTER'S CHART

LOCATION	DATE/TIME

COMMENTS
Found low down on trunks of oaks and Sweet Chestnut, this species causes a brown rot; the resulting stained timber is highly sought after by cabinet-makers.

SIZE Bracket width 1–5cm, depth 1mm

HABITAT On stumps and branches of oaks and Sweet Chestnut

STATUS Widespread and very common **FRUITING SEASON** Jan–Dec

KEY FACT Normally fairly easy to recognise with the naked eye, but there are times when it forms resupinate patches rather than brackets; in such cases a powerful hand lens is useful in detecting the minute hair-like projections on the fertile lower surface.

IDENTIFICATION

Forms densely crowded, tiered brackets. Individual brackets are very thin, rigid and wavy. Upper surface is concentrically zoned, the number of zones increasing with age; dark brown to almost black. Fertile lower surface is chocolate brown and covered in minute hair-like bristles.

COMMENTS

A common species that can be found at any time of year, especially on stumps and fallen branches of oaks and Sweet Chestnut.

SPOTTER'S CHART

LOCATION	DATE/TIME

TIGER'S EYE
Coltricia perennis

FACT FILE

SIZE **Cap diameter 3–8cm; height 1–4cm**
HABITAT **On acid sandy soils near pines** STATUS **Widespread and occasional** FRUITING SEASON **Aug–Nov**

IDENTIFICATION
Cap is flat to funnel-shaped, circular but usually with a wavy margin; upper surface is finely hairy, with well-defined concentric bands of brown and ochre; lower surface bears the tube layer, this a few millimetres thick and running down stem; pores tiny and greyish. Stem is central, tough, finely hairy, dark orange-brown.

KEY FACT
The habit of growing on soil, rather than wood, is unusual in polypores. To avoid confusion with some of the rare tooth fungi that also grow on soil, check the underside – tooth fungi have spines, not pores.

COMMENTS
An attractive species growing beside paths on heaths and moors singly or in small groups, and with adjacent caps sometimes fused.

SPOTTER'S CHART

LOCATION	DATE/TIME

FACT FILE SIZE Fruit-body width 2–7cm HABITAT On twigs and branches of various trees and shrubs STATUS Widespread and very common FRUITING SEASON Sep–Feb

IDENTIFICATION

Fruit body is convoluted, consisting of numerous folded lobes that can give it an almost brain-like appearance. Flesh is soft and jelly-like when moist, semi-translucent; bright yellow, fading to pale yellow or almost white after prolonged rain; shrivelling and hardening to deep yellow or orange on drying.

KEY FACT Yellow Brain is a parasite of *Peniophora* fungal species inhabiting the same twig or branch, although the host is not always in evidence. Other species of *Tremella* are also parasitic on other fungi.

COMMENTS

Although the species occurs on a wide range of trees and shrubs, it is probably most abundant on attached or fallen branches of gorse from late autumn through the winter.

SPOTTER'S CHART	
LOCATION	DATE/TIME

JELLY EAR
Auricularia auricula-judae

FACT FILE

SIZE Fruit-body width 3–8cm **HABITAT** On standing or fallen wood of many deciduous trees and shrubs
STATUS Widespread and very common **FRUITING SEASON** Jan–Dec

IDENTIFICATION
Fruit body is typically ear-shaped and gelatinous when fresh, shrivelling and hardening when dry. Attached to substrate via finely hairy cinnamon-brown outer surface. Inner surface is smooth to wrinkled and likened to a human ear, becoming more wrinkled with age; greyish brown.

KEY FACT
New fruit bodies are usually formed in winter, but they can persist throughout the year owing to their ability to survive prolonged desiccation in a hardened, rind-like state and reconstituting in wet weather.

SPOTTER'S CHART

LOCATION	DATE/TIME

COMMENTS
Although it occurs on a wide range of woody species, Jelly Ear seems to favour Elder; it can usually be found with relative ease by inspecting attached or fallen branches.

TRIPE FUNGUS
Auricularia mesenterica

FACT FILE SIZE Bracket length 2–6cm, width 1–3cm, depth 3–5mm HABITAT Dead wood of deciduous trees STATUS Widespread and common in England FRUITING SEASON Oct–Feb

IDENTIFICATION

Fruit bodies are resupinate or form gelatinous brackets in dense, overlapping tiers. Upper surface is hairy, undulating, with a lobed, wavy margin; concentrically banded in light grey and brown, or even green from algal staining. Lower surface has vein-like wrinkles; purple-brown, sometimes with a white bloom.

KEY FACT The upper surface often has a green tinge or zone from algae that have established on its surface, and the underside can sometimes have a white bloom caused by the release of millions of white spores.

COMMENTS

New brackets are usually formed in late autumn or winter on dead deciduous wood, especially stumps and fallen trunks of elms and Ash.

SPOTTER'S CHART

LOCATION	DATE/TIME

SILVERLEAF FUNGUS
Chondrostereum purpureum

FACT FILE

SIZE Bracket length 1–3cm, width 1–2cm, depth 2–3mm HABITAT Parasitic on deciduous trees STATUS Widespread and very common FRUITING SEASON Oct–Feb

IDENTIFICATION
Initially forms irregular, shapeless patches, vivid purple with a pale growing margin; later develops multiple small, wavy-edged, leathery brackets in dense, overlapping tiers. Upper surface is covered in whitish hairs. Lower surface is smooth, covered in minute pores; purple, becoming browner and eventually with no trace of purple.

SPOTTER'S CHART

LOCATION	DATE/TIME

COMMENTS
A common species that fruits afresh mainly from Nov, after which it is a conspicuous sight on stumps of various deciduous trees, especially birches.

KEY FACT
A serious pest of fruit trees and other members of the *Rosaceae* family, the species is initially parasitic and then saprotrophic. As its common name suggests, it causes the leaves of infected trees to turn silver.

FACT FILE

SIZE **Crust width 1–10cm** HABITAT **Dead wood of deciduous trees, especially Beech and birches** STATUS **Widespread and common** FRUITING SEASON **Oct–Feb**

IDENTIFICATION
Forms resupinate patches that may or may not merge into one another but never develop brackets. Surface is wrinkled, often radially from centre, sometimes knobbly; colour is variable, from bright orange through pinkish orange to greyish violet; margin is finely hairy.

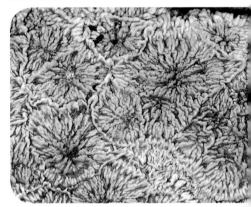

COMMENTS
A striking and beautiful species in its bright orange form, Wrinkled Crust often fruits along cracks and fissures in tree bark from late autumn to winter.

KEY FACT Owing to its wide range of colour forms, the species can be quite tricky to identify at times. The similar *Phlebia rufa* prefers oaks, is reddish brown and is never radially wrinkled.

SPOTTER'S CHART

LOCATION	DATE/TIME

JELLY ROT
Phlebia tremellosa

FACT FILE

SIZE Bracket length 2–6cm, width 1–4cm, depth 2–4mm HABITAT On fallen, decaying wood of deciduous trees STATUS Widespread and very common FRUITING SEASON Sep–Jan

IDENTIFICATION
Wholly resupinate or, more commonly, with a flimsy projecting bracket, sometimes covering extensive areas when multiple fruiting patches fuse; all parts are soft and gelatinous. Upper surface is covered in white hairs. Fertile lower surface is a complex network of ridge-like folds; yellowish, orangey or pinkish.

KEY FACT
Most other *Phlebia* species never form brackets and are totally resupinate, such as the Wrinkled Crust. This species, however, can sometimes form densely tiered brackets over quite large areas.

COMMENTS
Typically encountered freshly fruiting from mid-autumn to early winter, especially on fallen trunks and stumps of deciduous trees such as birches and Beech.

SPOTTER'S CHART

LOCATION	DATE/TIME

FACT FILE

SIZE **Bracket width 1–3cm, depth 2–4mm**
HABITAT **Associated with trees on acid sandy soils**
STATUS **Widespread and common** FRUITING SEASON **Sep–Feb**

IDENTIFICATION
Forms dense patches of fused and overlapping fan-like brackets. Upper surface is covered in coarse radiating fibres; dark chocolate brown, with a spiky white growing margin when fresh. Fertile lower surface is unevenly bumpy or warty, pale milky brown.

COMMENTS
Earthfan usually grows at ground level among moss or attached to bits of woody debris or stumps, but is not the easiest species to spot.

SPOTTER'S CHART

LOCATION	DATE/TIME

KEY FACT

This species forms a mycorrhizal association with the roots of various trees and is well known in conifer nurseries, where it often starts by forming a kind of collar around the stem base of young seedlings.

WOOD HEDGEHOG
Hydnum repandum

FACT FILE

SIZE Cap diameter 3–10cm; height 3–6cm
HABITAT Soil and leaf-litter, mainly in deciduous woods
STATUS Widespread and common **FRUITING SEASON** Sep–Dec

IDENTIFICATION
Cap is domed, sometimes developing a central depression, undulating and wavy-edged, margin inrolled; surface is suede-like, pale creamy yellow. Underside is covered in many fragile creamy spines or 'teeth' running decurrently down stem. Stem is sometimes off-centre, cylindrical, straight or bending, whitish.

KEY FACT
The give-away character of this species is the abundance of teeth on its underside. The Terracotta Hedgehog *Hydnum rufescens* also has teeth but is generally smaller, with a more orange cap.

SPOTTER'S CHART

LOCATION	DATE/TIME

COMMENTS
A good edible species occurring in the autumn singly or, more usually, in small groups or partial rings on the woodland floor.

HAIRY EARTHTONGUE
Trichoglossum hirsutum

FACT FILE

SIZE **Height 3–8cm** HABITAT **Mainly unimproved acidic grassland and dunes** STATUS **Widespread and common** FRUITING SEASON **Sep–Jan**

IDENTIFICATION

Fruit bodies are club- to spatula-shaped, entirely black. Fertile head is compressed, sometimes grooved, abruptly tapering into stem, with abundant tiny, fine bristles. Stem is cylindrical, covered in abundant projecting bristles that are more conspicuous than those on head and best viewed with a hand lens.

COMMENTS

The species usually occurs in groups in short turf, including lawns, in both lowland and upland areas in autumn.

KEY FACT

Although other species of *Trichoglossum* do exist in Britain they are quite rare, so this ascomycete is most likely to be confused with earthtongues in the genus *Geoglossum*, though these do not have a bristly stem.

SPOTTER'S CHART

LOCATION	DATE/TIME

JELLY BABIES
Leotia lubrica

FACT FILE

SIZE Head diameter 0.5–2cm; height 2–8cm
HABITAT Among moss and leaves in damp woodland
STATUS Widespread and common FRUITING SEASON Sep–Jan

IDENTIFICATION
Head is distinct from stem, convex, irregular, undulating, with a strongly inrolled and wavy margin, slimy when wet, yellowish to olive. Underside is more or less hidden from view but tapers seamlessly into stem. Stem is cylindrical or slightly compressed, rough from tiny pale greenish scales.

KEY FACT
Jelly Babies could be mistaken for a gill fungus, but on closer inspection no gills, pores or spines are visible. It is, in fact, an ascomycete, with the outer surface of the head bearing the asci.

COMMENTS
Normally gregarious and sometimes quite densely tufted; banks in damp woodland are a good place to search for it from around mid-autumn.

SPOTTER'S CHART

LOCATION	DATE/TIME

FACT FILE

SIZE **Diameter 1–4cm** HABITAT **Mainly fallen branches and trunks of oaks and Beech** STATUS **Widespread and very common** FRUITING SEASON **Sep–Feb**

IDENTIFICATION

Fruit body is initially entirely enclosed by scurfy brown outer skin, but gradually expands to reveal smooth, shiny black fertile inner surface of cup, before finally turning more or less inside out and becoming top-shaped. Flesh is gelatinous, rubbery. Spores are dark sooty brown.

COMMENTS

Typically found fruiting en masse on the upper surface of large, recently fallen branches of oaks and Beech, on which the bark is always still present.

KEY FACT

Although Black Bulgar is an ascomycete it could be confused with the basidiomycete Witches' Butter. However, it is firmer, the fertile surface is not covered in tiny pimples and the spores are black.

SPOTTER'S CHART

LOCATION	DATE/TIME

BEECH JELLYDISC
Neobulgaria pura

FACT FILE

SIZE Diameter 0.5–3cm HABITAT Mainly fallen
branches and trunks of Beech STATUS Widespread
and very common FRUITING SEASON Sep–Jan

IDENTIFICATION
Initially a tightly packed cluster of translucent ball-shaped fruit bodies
with a circular apical opening revealing the fertile cup. The cup gradually
opens out, flattening to become
disc-shaped or more leaf-shaped
and wavy-edged; flesh-coloured
with a hint of pink or lilac.
Flesh is gelatinous.

COMMENTS
Almost entirely restricted to
Beech, where large clusters of fruit
bodies commonly occur on fallen
trunks and branches in autumn.

KEY FACT

Being rather
variable in appearance, Beech
Jellydisc has the potential to
cause confusion. Fortunately,
however, the most similar
species in growth pattern and
habitat, the Black Bulgar, is
easily separated by colour alone.

SPOTTER'S CHART

LOCATION	DATE/TIME

FACT FILE
SIZE **Cup diameter 2–6mm; height 3–8mm**
HABITAT **On fallen and decaying wood of deciduous trees**
STATUS **Widespread and very common** FRUITING SEASON **Jan–Dec**

IDENTIFICATION

Fruit bodies are very small and flimsy, usually occurring gregariously on underside of wood. Cup is vaguely funnel-shaped, sometimes flattening and becoming wavy-edged; blue-green, like verdigris. Both upper and lower surfaces can become wrinkled, especially during drying. Stem is attached centrally or not.

COMMENTS

The fungus stains fallen wood green, which is what first attracts attention. Further examination may reveal the small fruit bodies being protected from desiccation on the wood underside.

KEY FACT
Infected oak, known as 'green oak', has been a popular wood to work down the ages. Pieces made from it are known as Tunbridge ware as its use originated in the Tunbridge Wells area.

SPOTTER'S CHART

LOCATION	DATE/TIME

WHITE SADDLE
Helvella crispa

FACT FILE

SIZE **Cap diameter 2–5cm; height 4–10cm**
HABITAT **On the ground in wooded areas, especially beside paths**
STATUS **Widespread and very common** FRUITING SEASON **Aug–Dec**

IDENTIFICATION
Cap is basically saddle-shaped but usually rather convoluted, with an undulating surface and irregularly lobed and sometimes ragged margin. Fertile upper surface is smooth, creamy white to pale buff. Lower surface is a shade darker. Stem is deeply longitudinally ribbed, hollow and often chambered.

KEY FACT This is one of a number of similar species, though it is unlikely to be confused on account of its larger size and colour. The Elfin Saddle *Helvella lacunosa* is also common and of a similar size, but is dark grey to black.

COMMENTS
Like a miniature work of art or small ornament, White Saddle is very common and fruits gregariously under trees along path edges and road verges.

SPOTTER'S CHART

LOCATION	DATE/TIME

FACT FILE   SIZE **Cup diameter 2–10cm** HABITAT **Bare soil or short turf, especially gravelly areas** STATUS **Widespread and common** FRUITING SEASON **Aug–Nov**

IDENTIFICATION

Fruit bodies occur singly or tightly clustered, and are vaguely cup-shaped but often warped and wavy-edged, flattening with age. Fertile upper surface is smooth, bright orange. Lower surface is covered in whitish down. Flesh is very thin and fragile, splitting easily. Stem is absent.

COMMENTS

An eye-catching species that generally occurs in groups and is best searched for on or beside gravel paths and rides in woods and heaths.

SPOTTER'S CHART

LOCATION	DATE/TIME

KEY FACT   In Britain, this is most likely to be confused with the **Orange Cup** *Melastiza chateri* and its relatives, though they are usually much smaller and have tiny hairs on the cup margin, visible with a hand lens.

CORAL SPOT
Nectria cinnabarina

SIZE Pustule diameter 0.5–2mm **HABITAT** Dead twigs of deciduous trees, especially Sycamore **STATUS** Widespread and very common **FRUITING SEASON** Jan–Dec

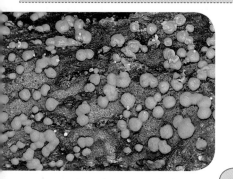

IDENTIFICATION
Infected sticks are either covered in pink spots, dark orange spots or a combination. On closer inspection, preferably with a hand lens, pink spots are seen to be swollen pustules and orange spots a cluster of tiny flask-shaped structures containing spores.

COMMENTS
It is found at any time of year, though probably more so in winter, when sticks with the bright pink and orange spots stand out against the otherwise drab woodland floor.

KEY FACT

The pink pustules form first and constitute the asexual (or conidial) stage. The dark orange flasks of the sexual stage form later, erupting from the exact same site as the pustules.

SPOTTER'S CHART

LOCATION	DATE/TIME

FACT FILE

SIZE **Height 5–15cm** HABITAT **Deciduous woods, gardens, dunes, woodchips, disturbed and burnt areas** STATUS **Widespread and occasional** FRUITING SEASON **Mar–May**

KEY FACT

The taxonomic status of this species is still in a state of flux. Many species of morel have been described over the years, but current opinion is most are merely forms of one highly variable species.

IDENTIFICATION

Head consists of a number of deep cells arranged in a somewhat distorted conical, oval or spherical honeycomb. Cells are variable, greyish brown, yellow or ochre with lighter or concolourous ribs. Stem is thickened at base, hollow, mealy, white.

COMMENTS

A well-known and highly prized edible, fruiting in spring and often faithfully on the same site for many years.

SPOTTER'S CHART

LOCATION	DATE/TIME

BLISTERED CUP
Peziza vesiculosa

SIZE Cup diameter 1–8cm HABITAT Dung heaps, rotting straw, mulch beds, woodchips STATUS Widespread and common FRUITING SEASON Jan–Dec **FACT FILE**

IDENTIFICATION

Fruit body is bladder-like with a narrow apical opening or more cup-shaped, often deformed and compressed from growing in tightly packed groups, margin becoming ragged. Fertile inner surface is smooth and shiny, yellowish brown. Outer surface is scurfy; buff, sometimes with darker brown scales. Flesh is relatively thick.

COMMENTS

Dung heaps containing horse manure and rotting straw are traditionally good places to find Blistered Cup, especially in winter. Woodchips can be equally productive.

KEY FACT

This species is set apart from other members in the genus by its bladder-shaped fruit bodies, which rarely expand or open out to become cup-shaped, and by having the thickest flesh of all.

SPOTTER'S CHART

LOCATION	DATE/TIME

FACT FILE

SIZE Cup diameter 2–5cm; height 3–10cm
HABITAT Mainly under deciduous trees, rarely under conifers
STATUS Widespread and common FRUITING SEASON Sep–Dec

KEY FACT When present, the pinkish tinge to the inner surface is a good indicator for this species, as is the overall yellow-orange colour and rusty spotting in older specimens.

IDENTIFICATION
Fruit body is an elongated, folded cup with a slit down one side, resembling an erect hare's ear. Inner surface is fertile, smooth, yellowish orange, often gaining a pink tinge and rusty spots with age. Outer surface is sterile, similarly coloured but without pink tones. Stem is rudimentary, white.

COMMENTS
A peculiar but lovely species that usually fruits with many 'pricked ears' clustered together, and that sometimes forms partial rings when multiple groups are present.

SPOTTER'S CHART

LOCATION	DATE/TIME

SCARLET ELFCUP
Sarcoscypha austriaca

FACT FILE

SIZE **Cup diameter 1–8cm** HABITAT **On rotting wood of deciduous trees in damp locations** STATUS **Widespread and very common** FRUITING SEASON **Jan–Apr**

KEY FACT *Sarcoscypha coccinea* grows in the same habitat at the same time of year and looks identical to the naked eye. A hand lens is required to see the straighter hairs on the outer surface to separate it from Scarlet Elfcup.

IDENTIFICATION
Fruit body is cup-shaped, expanding and becoming more open and saucer-shaped. Inner surface is fertile, smooth, bright scarlet. Outer surface is sterile, white to pale pinkish orange, with numerous fine curly hairs (hand lens required). Stem is continuous with outer surface, variable in length and often rooted in substrate.

COMMENTS
Appearing very early in the year, a group of this beautiful, striking species, fruiting on moss-covered logs, can brighten up the dullest of winter days.

SPOTTER'S CHART

LOCATION	DATE/TIME

FACT FILE

SIZE Height 3–7cm; width 1–3cm HABITAT On rotting, often buried wood of deciduous trees, especially Beech STATUS Widespread and very common FRUITING SEASON Aug–Dec

IDENTIFICATION

Fruit body is irregularly club- to finger-shaped with a rounded tip; surface is initially coated with a pale greyish bloom of asexual spores and has a white growing tip, later becoming finely pimpled and black all over. Stem is cylindrical and rooting. Flesh is tough, pure white.

KEY FACT The species undergoes two stages of development: the first produces asexual spores that appear as a grey bloom; and the second sees the ascospores maturing slowly and eventually cannoning from the now blackened, pimply surface.

COMMENTS

Fruits singly or in groups, when, as the common name suggests, it can look gruesomely like the charred fingers of a dead man poking out of the ground.

SPOTTER'S CHART

LOCATION	DATE/TIME

CANDLESNUFF FUNGUS
Xylaria hypoxylon

FACT FILE

SIZE Height 1–6cm HABITAT On stumps and rotting wood of deciduous trees STATUS Widespread and very common FRUITING SEASON Jan–Dec

IDENTIFICATION
Fruit body is variable, but most often branched to some degree and appearing antler-like. Initially dusted white from asexual spores (or conidia), the forked tips eventually disintegrate and whole fruit body becomes black and finely pimpled as asci from sexual stage develop. Flesh is tough, white.

KEY FACT
If a cross section is taken of the fruit body after it has fully matured, the flask-shaped structures containing the asci are just visible around the margin as black dots contrasting strongly with the white flesh.

COMMENTS
Extremely common and very conspicuous when the white 'antlers', present in its young conidial state, are fruiting en masse.

SPOTTER'S CHART

LOCATION	DATE/TIME

SIZE Diameter 2–10cm HABITAT Mainly on standing dead or dying Ash trees STATUS Widespread and very common FRUITING SEASON Jan–Dec

IDENTIFICATION

Fruit body is rounded, almost spherical but with a flatter underside against the substrate; initially reddish brown but blackening with age. Flesh is hard and composed of a number of concentric black and white growth layers, best seen when fungus is cut in half. Stem is absent.

SPOTTER'S CHART

LOCATION	DATE/TIME

KEY FACT

The species is also known as King Alfred's Cakes, after those said to have been burnt by the monarch. Interestingly, there are a number of other *Daldinia* species that do seem to have a preference for burnt wood.

COMMENTS

Ash trees are the place to find this species, where it is usually found growing in groups on dead or dying trunks and limbs.

INDEX

Common names are in plain text and scientific names are in *italic*.

PHOTOGRAPHIC ACKNOWLEDGEMENTS

Photographs supplied by Nature Photographers Ltd. All photographs by Paul Sterry except for those on the following pages:

S.C. Bisserot: 119; Andrew Merrick: 4, 12, 23, 24, 36, 57, 65, 72, 76, 79, 102, 108, 113, 114, 123, 126, 127, 135, 142, 143, 144, 151, 165, 170, 172 and cover photograph.